racquet made easy

Steve Lubarsky & Rod Delson with Jack Scagnetti

Published by
Melvin Powers
WILSHIRE BOOK COMPANY
12015 Sherman Road
No. Hollywood, California 91605
Telephone: (213) 875-1711

Printed by

HAL LEIGHTON PRINTING COMPANY
P.O. Box 3952
North Hollywood, California 91605
Telephone: (213) 983-1105

Library of Congress Catalog Card Number: 78-62721
Printed in the United States of America
ISBN 0-87980-361-4

CONTENTS

ACKNOWLEDGMENTS

The authors wish to express thanks for the friendship, inspiration and assistance, in the completion of this book, to the following:

Ron Botchan, Juanita Crockett, Ilana Hirsch, Sandy Kaufman, Morrie Lubarsky, Craig Scagnetti and Michael Mjehovich.

MEET THE AUTHORS

STEVE LUBARSKY

A graduate of the University of California at Santa Barbara with a B.A. in Social Sciences, Steve Lubarsky earned his elementary and junior high school teaching credentials in 1972 from California State University at San Jose. He began playing racquetball in 1970, earning recognition as a player, official and tournament director. In 1975 he became athletic director and director of membership at the Supreme Court Sports Center in San Jose and in 1977 he was named director of operations for the Supreme Court Sports Center in Ft. Lauderdale, Florida. He is currently general manager and co-owner of the Supreme Court Sports Center Racquetball Club in Van Nuys, California. In 1978 he was named to the Omega Sports Racquetball Advisory Staff and signed by Omega to be a member of their playing staff.

ROD DELSON

A graduate of the University of California at Santa Barbara with a B.A. in social sciences, Rod Delson earned his high school teaching credential in 1971 at UC-Santa Barbara. He began playing racquetball in 1968 and became known as a player, official and tournament director. In 1975 he became manager of the Supreme Court Sports Center Racquetball Club in San Jose, California, and in 1978 he was named director of operations for the Supreme Court Center in Palo Alto, California. Currently he is co-owner and manager of the Santa Monica Racquetball Club in California. In 1978 he was named to the AMF-Voit Racquetball Advisory Staff.

JACK SCAGNETTI

A former newspaper sports reporter and columnist, and managing editor of a weekly newspaper, Jack Scagnetti worked for several years as a public relations director, promoter and business manager of a private athletic and social club in Detroit. Moving to California in 1958, he became promotion director for a chain of bowling centers. From 1966-1968 he served as editorial director of a group of national automotive magazines. Since 1968 he has been a free-lance writer and photographer, authoring nearly 1,000 magazine articles and 11 books, five of the books on how-to techniques in sports subjects.

Steve Lubarsky

Rod Delson

FOREWORD

Racquetball's rapid growth the past decade can be attributed to the fact it provides a good physical and mental workout, is easy to learn, is a family type sport, enjoyable at many age levels, is inexpensive, and fun.

My involvement during this time has been as a tournament player and teaching professional. The teaching experience has been in two diverse environments: 1) at the club level, where conditions are ideal and 2) the collegiate ranks, where time, space and equipment are limited. The differing challenges have proven invaluable in developing a broader foundation of teaching techniques.

Some time ago, Steve Lubarsky and Rod Delson approached me concerning the lack of a functional racquetball text book that could be utilized in instruction at the club level as well as in a school class program. I agreed that there certainly was a need for this type of instructional material.

After reading the manuscript of this book by Steve and Rod, I was pleased to see that it is a text that can be used in all teaching situations. Their explanations of fundamentals and techniques are written in terms that both the novice and advanced player can easily comprehend. Moreover, the text is supported by fine illustrations that fully explain the game.

Lubarsky and Delson, both graduates of the University of California (Santa Barbara) with degrees in physical education, are former school teachers. In recent years they have been serving as managers of large,

Foreword

modern racquetball clubs. They have played in tournaments, and organized and officiated tournaments. They know ever facet of the game.

They have utilized their overall experience in racquetball and the teaching profession to compile this book, which I know will be a great aid to instructors and students. I am honored to write this foreword.

—RON BOTCHAN
Professor of Physical Education, M.A.,
Los Angeles City College

NOTE: Ron Botchan, former professional football player with the San Diego Chargers and Houston Oilers, is a racquetball professional at the Supreme Court, Van Nuys, California, a member of the AMF-Voit Racquetball Advisory Staff and the 1978 California State Seniors Racquetball champion.

RON BOTCHAN

Chapter 1

THE GAME AND ITS HISTORY

Racquetball, as it is played today, is a comparatively new sport. Formally organized in 1968, it is a game that has attracted millions of physical-fitness-minded men, women and children throughout North America.

Racquetball's appeal is attributed to the fact that it is a game offering a person an enjoyable physical and mental workout without requiring a high degree of skill. Anyone who has a general degree of motor ability—men, women, boys and girls—can play racquetball and enjoy it.

Racquetball evolved directly from the game of paddleball, which was originated in the 1920's by Earl Riskey of the University of Michigan. As he watched tennis players practice their strokes in a handball court, he conceived the idea that one could play a game similar to handball that would also include the skills of tennis. The game became known as paddleball because a wooden paddle was used. Tennis players found it a good way to better their skills. Paddleball soon grew in popularity and was given a big boost during World War II when it was selected as one of the activities in the U.S. Armed Forces Conditioning Program held at the University of Michigan. It became a favorite sport with the military, and after the war they continued to play the game in their communities.

Handball players, particularly older players, took up paddleball as they found it gave them a good workout, was enjoyable, and easier on the hands.

In 1949, Joe Sobek, who had left his profession as a tennis and squash professional, was observing paddleball played by members of the Greenwhich, Connecticut YMCA. Sobek concluded that the game would be more interesting if a strung racket were used rather than the solid-faced wood version. He designed a racket and had it manufactured by a New England racket maker and soon started a group of men playing the new version of paddleball. It was called paddle rackets. Early rules were based primarily on established squash rules. The sport eventually spread nationwide, mostly played at YMCA's and other community gymnasiums.

As the game grew in popularity, under such names as paddle tennis, paddleball and paddle rackets, nationwide competition emerged. A National Paddleball Association was formed in 1967 and the group staged its first tournament in Milwaukee on May 23-26, 1968, calling it the National Paddleball Tournament. It attracted 72 entries from all over the United States and some from Canada.

In 1969 the organization changed its name to International Racquetball Association. The word paddle was dropped because it appeared to denote the use of a wooden paddle. The first International Racquetball Association championship tournament, held in St. Louis, in 1969, attracted entries from many states.

Racquetball players began crowding handball courts and this caused a severe backlash from oldtime handball players as there was already a shortage of handball courts. Faced with this problem, it was obvious that the solution was to build racquetball facilities, and by the mid-1970's modern buildings were constructed featuring handball and racquetball playing areas. More and more handball players began taking up racquetball.

More and more women also expressed interest in racquetball and their participation played a vital role in the sport's growth. With women, came more children to play the game. Women insisted on more colorful clothing, and the apparel manufacturers took the cue and introduced handsome and comfortable uniforms for both men and women. Women particularly enjoyed the sport because it was a game they could play with their sons and daughters and husbands. The physical and social benefits of racquetball appealed to women. Racquetball burned up calories, toned muscles and relieved tension.

As the game developed, the equipment and playing facilities became more sophisticated. By the early 1970's, equipment manufacturers began making improvements in the racquetball racquets. Wooden-framed racquets, which were bulky and heavy and could result in sore arms and injuries, were replaced by aluminum racquets and fiberglass or plastic mixed

Racquetball is an ideal sport in which women can play with men or compete against them. Physical and social benefits are plentiful.

with fiberglass. Frames became lighter and much easier to swing. Moreover, the strings used for racquets were of better quality and were strung looser than before, resulting in improved control without as much power required. A lively ball was developed, speeding up the game.

Playing facilities were upgraded and several with a country club atmosphere were built in areas around the country. The air conditioned courts—featuring racquetball, handball and paddleball—include such facilities as a pro shop, sauna, steam and jacuzzi, snack and refreshment bar, lounge areas, lockers and showers, and viewing gallery. Glass-walled courts provide easier viewing at some courts. Lessons, clinics, and tournaments are featured.

Racquetball can be learned in a few lessons (most players enjoy some degree of success in their first try). Rules are easy to learn, and the sport requires a minimum of equipment.

Racquetball is played in a 20x20-foot-high, 40-foot-long court. It's fast moving, very similar to handball and tennis. Like handball, it's played against the wall. Like ping-pong, the game is won by the first player to reach 21 points. The best two-out-of-three games wins the match.

One player, standing in the serving zone, bounces the ball in front of his or her body. He or she then hits it against the front wall in a manner that will cause it to bounce back anywhere past the short line, with or without hitting a side wall. The opponent must return the ball to the front wall on a fly before it hits the floor twice, hitting it either before it bounces once on the floor or before it bounces at all. The opponent may use any combination of walls and ceiling in returning the ball, as long as it eventually hits the front wall before bouncing on the floor. Should the ball fail to hit the front wall or isn't returned before it bounces on the floor twice, the server wins a point and continues to serve.

If the server loses the exchange, the server loses the serve (points are awarded exclusively to the server as in volleyball).

Each player's objective is to hit the ball to an area of the court where the opponent isn't, thus retaining the serve and scoring points.

That's all there is to the sport, except for certain rules (which are included in this book) and courtesies, such as no tripping or blocking your opponent's shot, and certain strategies (which are described elsewhere in this book).

The combination of healthful exercise, recreation, concentration and competition in a swift-moving, muscle-toning game that provides a challenge for mind and body while having fun makes racquetball a sport

6

Instructor shows student how to hit out in front at knee height and where to make proper contact on the racquet.

Instructor shows student how to bring a backhand swing straight and level across her body.

most anyone will enjoy.

Today racquetball is played by more than 5,000,000 Americans, perhaps a third of them women. Two professional circuits are helping to increase racquetball's popularity. Some of the professional players are earning very handsome salaries. Racquetball's fast-moving action has attracted television coverage.

Racquetball is truly a lifetime sport, and that in itself will make it a sport that is here to stay and grow.

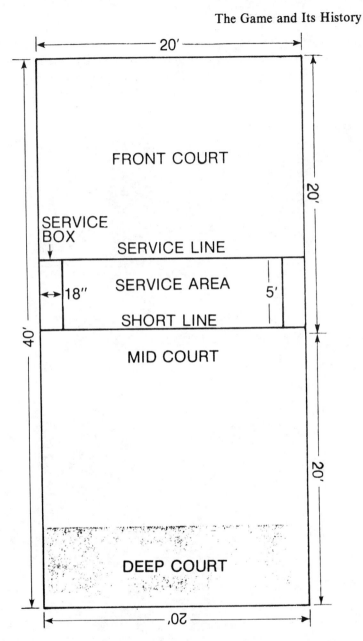

Standard four-wall racquetball court is 20 feet wide, 20 feet high and 40 feet long, with a back wall at least 12 feet high. It's divided into a front court and a back court by a short line. Five feet in front of the short line is the service line.

9

Doubles play is becoming increasingly popular. At most racquetball clubs, organized doubles play is an important part of the program.

Chapter 2

CHOOSING EQUIPMENT

One of the major reasons racquetball has grown so rapidly in popularity is that it requires very little equipment and it takes comparatively far less money to outfit a player.

Start by selecting a comfortable T-shirt, shorts and white socks. If racquetball represents your return to a physical fitness program, you may be more comfortable wearing two pairs of socks because your feet will probably not be conditioned to running and this will help avoid blisters or skin irritations. Cotton socks, usually the type referred to as sanitary socks, are best for wearing under your regular socks. Both types of socks are available at sporting goods stores or your club's pro shop.

Selecting proper shoes is very important in racquetball. Due to the similarity of movement and type of wooden floor, any good basketball-racquetball-volleyball shoe will do. They are available at a wide range of prices. Do not skimp when buying shoes. The better the shoe the longer it will last and the more comfortable you'll be while wearing it.

Check shoes for three important features before you buy them: 1) a well-structured arch support; 2) a sturdy but comfortable heel cup and 3) a reinforced rubber tip.

The continual lateral movement on the court can cause the front of a shoe to receive such excessive wear that the shoe will need replacing in a relatively short time. A good quality shoe will last as long as several inexpensive pairs, and at the same time you can be playing comfortably and safely.

Perhaps your most difficult decision will be determining which racquet you should buy. Sporting goods stores and racquetball pro shops offer a wide variety of racquets in both aluminum and fiberglass construction.

We always have the new player take two or three of the inexpensive racquets and swing them back and forth. We then ask the player to choose the racquet that feels the most fluid and well balanced. Each racquet has its weight distributed differently and no racquet is more properly balanced than another.

Choose the racquet which feels the most comfortable and well balanced to you. A beginner usually asks us: "Which racquet do you like?" We tell them that doesn't matter—"you're personal preference is just as valid."

We do offer three tips in choosing a racquet:

1) Never choose a wooden racquet as it is heavy and dangerous on the court. Your arm will tire easily and should the wooden racquet hit the wall or floor, it will easily splinter. Wooden racquets are a reminder of the early days of racquetball when it was commonly confused with paddle ball. Warping is also common with wooden racquets. Keep in mind, too, that most clubs will not allow wooden racquets to be used on their courts.

2) Choose an inexpensive racquet if you are a beginner. As you become accustomed to the game, your needs in a racquet may change.

3) Choose a racquet made by a company that offers some type of warranty. Aluminum racquets will generally be guaranteed for a longer period of time than fiberglass.

Aluminum and fiberglass racquets each have their good points and, thus, some players are usually seen playing with only one type. Aluminum racquets are more durable and provide greater power due to greater weight and more rigid construction. Although the two racquets may only be five to 10 grams apart in weight, you will be able to feel this difference in your arm after the first game of your set.

The fiberglass racquet offers players greater control. Because of the nature of fiberglass, it has more flexibility than aluminum. This means that the ball will stay on the face of the racquet for a longer period of time and, therefore, is easier to guide during the stroke.

Most clubs will emphasize the importance of wearing something to protect the eyes. Eye guards are available today at very reasonable prices. Your eyes are the only vulnerable part of your body subject to harm on the court. No player should play without eye protection.

There are some optional items of equipment that some players may want

Racquetball clothes are stylish and comfortable, and along with the equipment, comparatively inexpensive. Some players wear protective eye glasses.

while others can do without. These include wrist bands, head bands, elbow and knee pads, and a glove. Purchase of any of these items is a matter of personal choice.

Although racquetball is well established, it is still in its infancy and it will not be surprising to see changes in equipment trends as is evident in most comparatively new sports. New styles especially designed for racquetball clothes emerged in 1977-78 and more are on the way. For example, since racquetball involves a lot of sweating, new racquetball attire today includes loose mesh sleeveless shirts with terrycloth inserts across the chest for wiping sweating palms. There are also unlined gym trunks made of terrycloth for absorption of sweat.

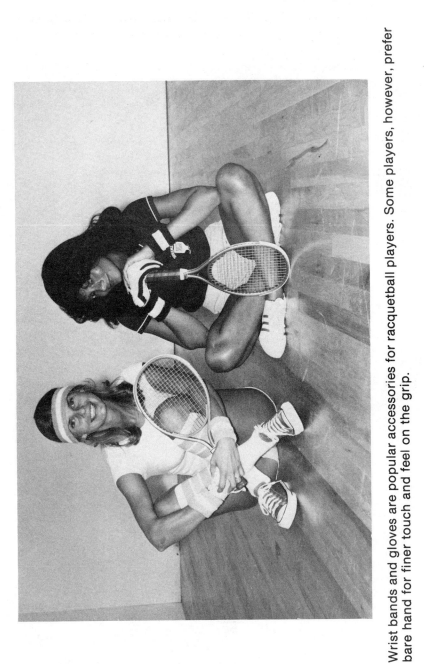

Wrist bands and gloves are popular accessories for racquetball players. Some players, however, prefer bare hand for finer touch and feel on the grip.

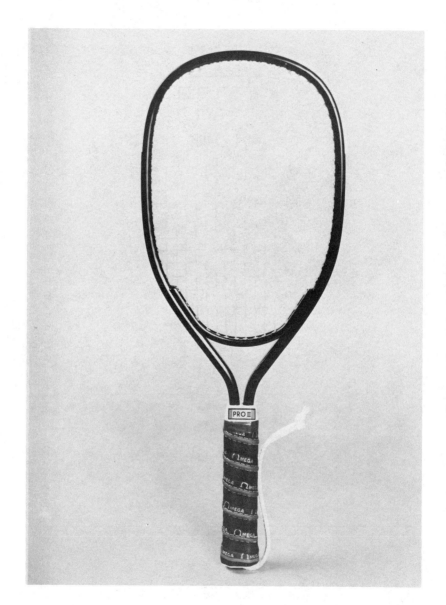

Racquets come in advanced designs nowadays. Omega's Pro-II has a computer-designed aluminum frame and raised leather grip.

Omega's Spoiler racquet, ideal for juniors and beginners, has a light-weight, carbon-black, glass-filled one-piece nylon frame.

Racquetball involves many lateral movements which necessitate that a player wear good shoes with a well-structured arch support, sturdy but comfortable heel cup and reinforced rubber tip.

17

Chapter 3

PREPARING TO PLAY

Because the sport of racquetball has grown so fast, the vital role of conditioning and exercising in preparation of play has not been truly emphasized as much as it should.

Racquetball can be considered somewhat paradoxical in that it's played by the recreation-minded casual athlete seeking a fast work-out to keep in good physical condition, but requires the flexibility, strength and stamina of most competitive sports. Thus, whether you are the tournament-minded player or the casual recreational player, you should follow a regular pre-game exercise and conditioning schedule.

There are certain things all players should do before they serve their first ball. A good pre-game warmup is important not only to enable you to give a better performance on the court, but to avoid possible injury. It doesn't matter whether you play once a week or seven times a week, you need to exercise before you begin play.

The objective of your pre-game exercise period should be that you will be in proper physical condition to react to the first serve as though you were in your second game.

You should always start your exercises slowly, avoiding any jerky motions. Think of your muscles as a rubber band. Smooth, easy motions will allow great flexibility, but a quick snap may cause the rubber band to break. This is usually the cause of sprained or pulled muscles. Go through a warmup at a pace that is comfortable to you, but be thorough.

From personal experience and from observing and talking to experienced, competent racquetball players, we have selected exercises that are essential in avoiding injury and enhancing performance. While you may not be able to fully complete each exercise in the beginning, a few weeks of continual effort will enable you to perform to par. Let's take a look at these vital exercises:

JUMPING JACKS

Begin this exercise with your feet together and hands at your sides. Clap your hands together over your head as you jump and spread your legs apart. Return to your starting position. Two intervals of 25 jumps will set your respiratory and cardiovascular system in motion. Breathe easy and maintain a steady pace.

TOE TOUCH / KNEE BEND

Place your feet together and put your hands on your hips. Bend over and touch the floor in front of your toes. Return to the erect position and then bend at your knees until you are in a crouch position (similar to a catcher in baseball). Then, once again, return to the erect position. Concentrate on keeping your posture erect and your legs straight when stretching. Repeat this exercise in 15 evenly-paced motions.

ALTERNATING TOE TOUCH

Spread your legs apart approximately three to six inches beyond your shoulders. Touch your right toe with your left hand. Return to the erect position and then touch your left toe with your right hand. Repeat this exercise until you have touched each foot 15 times.

HIP SWIVEL

This exercise features four bouncy movements. Begin by standing erect with your hands on your hips. Then, keeping your legs straight, bend forward with your upper body. Return your upper body slightly up and bend to the side, repeating the motion and bending to the other side until you have completed a full circle bend in each direction. Do this in intervals of 10 complete circles.

Workouts in an exercise room, which most racquetball clubs include, are very helpful. Wrist-curl exercise aids in developing quick wrist snap.

SHOULDER CIRCLES

Stand erect with your arms extended outward and parallel to the ground. Keep your arms extended and move them simultaneously in a circular motion. Do 10 circles forward and then 10 circles backward. Pause for 10 seconds and repeat the exercise.

BASEBALL THROW

Throw the ball against the front wall in a baseball style 10 times, first with your stroking arm and then with your other arm. Step forward with each throw.

This pull-down exercise will strengthen arms and shoulders. Modern racquetball centers usually have a full line of exercise equipment.

Bench press exercise helps to develop shoulders, arms and wrists for extra power into shotmaking.

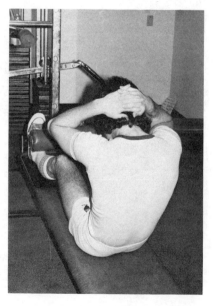

Situps are an ideal exercise for loosening up muscles. They will trim your waistline and give you stronger stomach muscles.

SIDE SHUFFLE

Stand near the back of the court, as you would if you were awaiting your opponent's serve. Position yourself in a crouch, similar to that of a shortstop awaiting a pitch. Slide or shuffle your feet to the right three times, then back to your starting point and continue three more times to the left for a total of six shuffles. Continue this exercise until you have moved to the right and left five times each. Rest 20 seconds and repeat the drill.

The aforegoing exercises will take between 10 to 15 minutes. Those few minutes will greatly decrease your chance of injury and increase your potential for better performance on the court.

The amount of additional conditioning you pursue should be determined by the level of play you wish to achieve. A casual player may not choose any additional exercise programs, but the determined player will rely upon it. The player who plans to compete in tournaments, whether on the club or regional level, will want to add conditioning drills to his or her schedule.

Since the legs and the cardio-vascular system are so important in racquetball, jogging is a very good exercise. Find a place to jog that is on soft dirt or grass. Cement and asphalt are an unnecessary shock to your ankles, knees and hips. At the end of your jog, pace off about 100 yards. Then, at three-quarter speed, run the 100 yards. Walk back to where you began and repeat this 10 times. On your last two runs you should be running at full speed. Jog and walk another half mile and you have completed your workout.

It is recommended that you run a minimum of one to three miles.

Another excellent form of exercise is working out with weights. Use a weight you can lift smoothly and in an evenly paced manner rather than one that may cause jerky and irregular motions.

The following exercises will be very helpful:

1) Bench press
2) Military press
3) Rowing exercise
4) Curls for the biceps
5) Wrist curls

We will not detail these exercises, as the style and intervals or amount of weight used will greatly vary among individuals, as will the type of weight training equipment utilized. Consult someone experienced in weight training. We have not included weight training exercises involving the legs because jogging will provide you with all the leg conditioning you'll need.

Hip swivel exercise, with a full circle bend in each direction, is good for increasing spinal flexibility.

A quick pre-game exercise to loosen muscles is bending and alternating touching each toe.

Quick warmups can be done to stretch and loosen up leg muscles before beginning play.

Overhead shoulder press is an excellent exercise to strength-en biceps, shoulders and triceps for added hitting power.

It's a good idea to stretch your legs from side to side with lateral movements just before beginning play.

Toe touch/knee bend exercise is excellent for loosening up. After bending and touching floor in front of toes, return to erect position and then bend at your knees until you are in a crouch position.

Racquetball is played by the recreation-minded casual athlete seeking a fast work-out to keep fit, but requires flexibility, strength and stamina of most competitive sports.

Chapter 4

GRIPS AND BASIC STROKES

In racquetball, there are well-defined basic fundamentals to learn if you desire to understand the concept of the game, improve rapidly and have fun. The sport will be more enjoyable if you learn to play properly at the very beginning.

As a beginner, your success should be gauged by your own improvement and not by the number of points scored in your game. You should be concerned with learning properly—not winning. Sometimes you may find it beneficial to play against someone and not keep score. Once you have mastered the basic fundamentals and are ready to test your skill, you will find many players eager to give you the opportunity for competition and you can focus on winning.

As a beginner, your own discipline and patience are vital to your development as a good player. As you progress through this book, the strategy and techniques we emphasize will become very logical and you will have a better understanding of why we stress specific ideas and drills.

Don't look for easy shots or your own quick method of strategy. We have observed many beginners and, supposedly, intermediate players who flail themselves around the court, denying themselves and their partners of fully grasping the fundamentals and the enjoyment of the sport. You can become a successful participant in a short time if you will let logic and patience guide you. Fifty per cent of all learning can be achieved through comprehension of the material presented in this book, and the remaining

50 per cent is the application of this material.

Take yourself step by step through this book and do not become discouraged if you don't quickly master a fundamental. Be patient. Discipline yourself to practice and you'll soon see improvement.

THE GRIP

As in golf or tennis, a good grip is a prime requisite for good performance in racquetball. Begin by holding the racquet out in front of you with your off hand on the top of the racquet and the base of the handle against your stomach. Place your hand on the face, touching the strings, and slide your hand down the racquet along the handle. When your small finger is approximately three quarters of an inch from the end of the racquet, stop. The space between your thumb and index finger, which looks like a "V," should be directly in line with the edge of the racquet. Next, move your index finger forward, as though you were gripping the trigger of a gun. This "trigger" grip will allow you greater control of where you want to hit the ball.

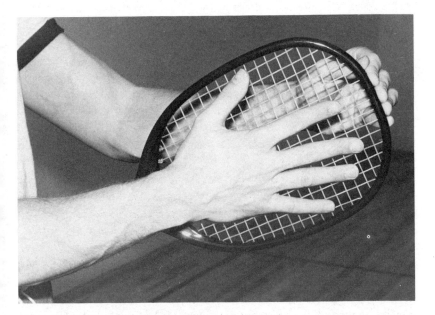

For starting a firm, handshake grip, place your hand on the face of the racquet, touching the strings, and slide your hand down the racquet along the handle.

Grips and Basic Strokes

A proper grip is with the space between your thumb and index finger, which looks like a V, directly in line with the edge of the racquet.

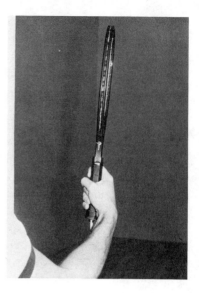

Side view of grip shows extended index finger for trigger-like hold to assure better control of strokes.

If the racquet feels unbalanced in your hand, you can remedy this by moving the racquet back and forth with your wrist until the racquet seems secure and evenly balanced in your hand.

There are three basic things to note in your grip:

1) The "V" should go up the edge of the racquet.

2) Your small finger should be three quarters of an inch from the base.

3) Your index finger should be extended.

Next, place your hand through the thong provided for the safety of you and your opponent, and grip the racquet.

As a beginner, you should use the same grip for your backhand as your forehand. You have enough to occupy your mind just in learning the proper fundamentals and the quick pace of the game.

The intermediate player may decide that a slight variation in the backhand grip will be beneficial. However, this should only be considered when you are able to determine the path of the ball (whether it comes off your racquet or that of your opponent) and its velocity. This variation in the grip is used to help make the contact between the ball and the racquet as flat as possible. However, at times, even the most proficient players will not

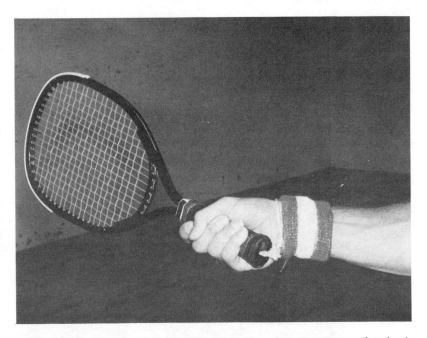

Grip the racquet approximately one half to three quarters of an inch from the end of the handle.

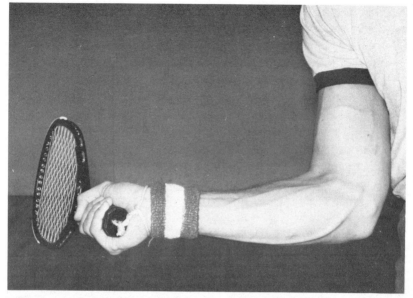

This shows position of racquet before and after contact with the ball. Note how wrist is snapped and rolled for added power.

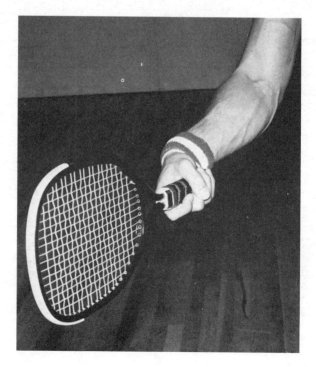

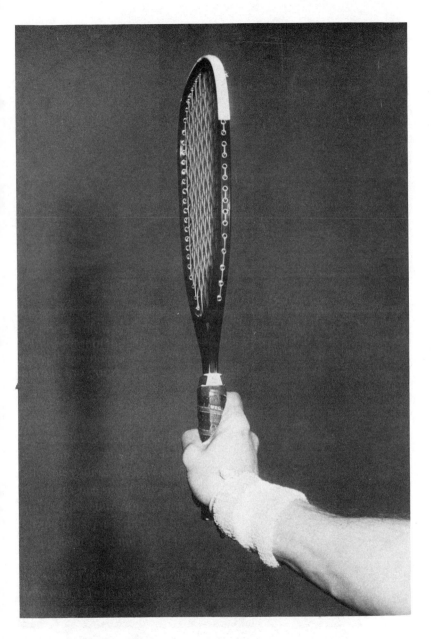

Backhand grip adjustment is achieved by rolling your grip counter-clockwise approximately three quarters of an inch over the top of the racquet.

Keep your arm in close to your body, always in the ready position.

have time to alter their grip. Therefore, it is essential to master the one-grip fundamental.

The backhand adjustment is achieved by rolling your grip counterclockwise, approximately three quarters of an inch over the top of the racquet. When you are involved in close-in rallies, you may not have time to adjust your wrist. When this occurs, try to angle your arm in such a manner as to keep your point of contact with the ball as flat as possible.

Racquetball is one of the few sports in which you can improve your play by observing the game in action. Do not be concerned with form or shot selection (unless you are in the finals of a tournament) but study the path of the ball. The greater your level of competency in reacting to the ball, the more time you will have to make any adjustments in your grip.

THE STROKE

In golf and tennis, you will note that certain players make the game appear very simple. This is the result of their understanding of the game and reacting in fluid motions, free from jerky or contorted action. The same is true in racquetball.

The forehand and backhand strokes are very similar to each other. The forehand is always easier to execute for the same reason that it is easier to throw a baseball with one arm compared to the other. We recommend that you concentrate solely on the forehand until you have an awareness of the six fundamentals of the stroke. When you begin to feel confident in your ability to make contact properly, you may then decide to start work on your backhand. The six basic fundamentals of the stroke are:

1) Keep your arm in close to your body. Squash players have been taught to do this by strapping a belt around their bicep and chest. While this type of discipline may not be necessary in racquetball, the concept should continually be emphasized.

2) In making contact with the ball when it is out in front of you, you must step into the ball—similar in execution to hitting a baseball.

3) Your point of contact with the ball should be at waist high; that is, the height of the ball when it is parallel to hips as you are stepping into the ball. This is usually six inches lower than waist high when you are standing erect. However, intermediate players will strive to hit the ball when it is on an even level with their knees.

4) Always swing level. A low shot is not the result of a downward stroke but is the direct result of an extension of a parallel line from the point of

Ideal point of contact with the ball for beginners should be at waist high level as you step into the ball. However, intermediate players will strive to hit the ball when it's on an even level with their knees. Experienced players can hit it effectively at ankle height.

contact of your shot and the wall.

5) As you make contact with the ball, remember to roll your wrist and snap it. The power in a shot does not come from raring back and flailing at the ball. Power is a combination of the strength in the step from your lead leg and the velocity of the snap of your wrist upon contact with the ball.

6) Always follow through with your swing. Avoid any chopping motions. If you want to hit the ball powerfully or are attempting a soft-touch shot, you will vary the velocity of your wrist action, but never alter your follow-through.

Learning what to do when you are not in position to set-up properly for a shot is something that comes with practice and experience. You must learn to discipline yourself to set-up so you can react to the ball rather than altering your form due to the location of the ball.

Whenever you follow these basic fundamentals, you are increasing your potential to execute a good shot. It is somewhat simple to follow these steps when practicing by yourself or rallying with an opponent before a game. It becomes a little more difficult when your are in competition and points are at stake. But be patient and maintain a confident attitude and you soon will find you have mastered these techniques.

INCORRECT

Correct way to step forward into a backhand shot is with your lead leg; using the opposite leg to step forward ruins body fluidity.

CORRECT

Chapter 5

SERVES

Beginners and many intermediate players fail to understand the impact the serve has upon the game. It is not unusual for a player to become so distracted on accumulating points that the effort it took to gain control of the serve is soon neglected.

The serve does not simply begin a rally; it is an offensive weapon that will set the play in action. When you are on the service line, you are controlling the tempo of the game and this is your opportunity to score points and win. It is vital that, as you learn the basic serves, you gain more than just an understanding of how to hit the ball. You must become aware of the different mode of play each serve sugeests. Once you have mastered the techniques involved with each serve, you can become as selective and cunning as a baseball pitcher who tries to outguess and manipulate the batter.

It is the objective of each serve to either make it impossible for your opponent to return the serve, or to force him or her to shoot an off-balanced return in an effort to keep the ball in play. If your serve fails to do either of the aforementioned, your opponent should be left with a serve that only permits a defensive maneuever, similar to that of hitting a safety in billiards. Thus, any type of aggressive return on your opponent's part would be a very low percentage shot.

Let's take a look at the basic serves, how to execute them, and their objectives:

THE LOB

The lob should always begin with yourself positioned in the middle of the service box. You should hit the ball on an angle that will place the ball in line with the back corner. If you've had some billiards experience, this will be easily understood. If this type of geometric play is new to you, then picture a point directly in the middle of the court. In order to hit the ball so that it strikes the front wall and bounces in line with your opponent's lefthand corner, your spot will be approximately 12 inches to the left of the middle. Now, with that spot in mind, move it up the front of the wall so that you are focusing on a point about 12 to 14 feet from the floor. Extend your arm in front of you and gently bounce the ball on the floor. As the ball bounces upward, step in line with the point on the wall and make contact with the ball at shoulder height.

Keep in mind that you will be hitting this serve with the ball in front of you and hitting it on a line which connects the ball to the point on the front wall. Do not look to see where the ball is going. If you hit the ball when it is in front of you, step into the ball and follow through, you will be able to clearly see the path of the ball. Bring your swing across your body. Remember to roll your wrist as you make contact with the ball, in the manner discussed earlier in hitting the forehand shot. The only difference in the wrist action of the lob serve will be the velocity in which you roll your wrist. You should want to hit the ball so that after it has struck the front wall, it will bounce softly and seem to drop or die as it approaches the back wall. Therefore, make a stroke that is about 2/5ths the velocity of the basic forehand shot.

When executed properly this shot will force your opponent deep into the back corner of the court. As you become more familiar with this serve, begin to modify the arc the ball takes. You can do this by adjusting the height of the point on the wall and the velocity of your wrist action. You will know you have begun to understand the basics of this serve when you begin to feel that you can control this serve just as easily as adjusting the height of a kite in the air.

Each serve you learn can be modified over a wide spectrum. Once you truly understand the logistics and mood involved with each serve, you will have a countless number of serves to use. You can become very experimental and creative with the understanding of each new serve. It is very important to learn to hit the serve to each corner — not only because not all

This player knows the importance of looking back at her opponent to see foe's position and, therefore, help determine type of serve.

In making a lob serve, as the ball bounces upward, step in line with the point on the wall and make contact with the ball at shoulder height. Be sure to follow through.

players are righthanded but the larger your repertoire of serves the greater the effectiveness of your serves. Your opponent will not be able to anticipate the path of the ball until after the ball is already in flight.

THE DRIVE SERVE

Like the lob serve, the drive serve is also begun from a position in the middle of the service box. The angle you will pattern your ball will be exactly the same as the lob serve. You should drop the ball out in front of you. Note that we have not said bounce the ball. Bouncing the ball is not necessary. You do not need any extra height as you did with the lob serve. As the ball comes up from the floor, your contact point will be on a line parallel with the floor and at knee height as you step into the ball. You should use a quick-snap action with your wrist as you make contact with the ball.

This serve will be most effective when it comes off the front wall with a crisp action. Many inexperienced players will flail themselves at the ball in an attempt to put power into this serve. Remember, the power needed from this stroke comes from the step into the ball and the velocity of the snap of your wrist. If you hit it properly, the ball will shoot into the corner without hitting the sidewall, and will strike the corner and die.

It is an especially effective serve against an opponent who has difficulty hitting the ball on the run, moves awkwardly laterally or who is tired. It forces your opponent to jump quickly into the mode of play you have established. This serve can also have many variations. You may try serving the ball so it will hit the sidewall just before it reaches the corner. As you become more proficient, you may decide to make contact with the ball at ankle height. Think of the many possibilities. This is a fast serve. If your opponent falters, for just one second, you may win a point without having to make contact with the ball again during that rally.

Notice that the lob and drive serves both started from the center of the court. Thus, your opponent has no knowledge of which serve you have chosen to execute until the ball is already in its flight. The longer it takes your opponent to learn the type of serve you have selected to use, the shorter the time for him or her to react.

THE LOW Z SERVE

This serve will be hit from a point midway between the sidewall and the center of the court. Again, the ball should be dropped in front of you. Make

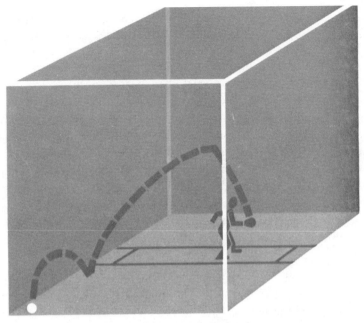

In hitting a low lob serve, hit the ball on an
angle that will place the ball in line with
the back corner. Lob generates slower-
paced game.

contact with the ball at knee height. You will want the path of the ball to hit
the front wall about six to eight inches from the sidewall. Remember to step
to the direction you want the ball to take and concentrate on keeping your
eye on the ball. The ball will strike the front wall, bounce to the sidewall,
come across the court. After bouncing, it will hit into the back of the sidewall and drop or die. If the ball is hit hard enough, after it hits the back sidewall, it may take an unpredictable bounce and strike the back wall or pop
out from the sidewall parallel with the back wall. The unpredictability
involved with this serve comes from the spin the ball acquires from the
initial action of the front wall-sidewall contact. This serve can be greatly
modified by just varying the angle you have chosen to hit the front wall by
just an inch and by a slight adjustment in the velocity of the wrist snap.

This serve, similar to the drive serve, focuses on a quick committing
response from your opponent. If he or she is not on top of this serve from
the very beginning, the returnee will be out of position and be chasing the
ball.

45

THE HIGH Z SERVE

The high Z serve is also set into motion from a point midway between the sidewall and the middle of the court. It's similar to the lob serve in that you slightly bounce the ball and make contact with it at a point just under shoulder height. Although the characteristics of this serve are somewhat similar to the lob, you will want the ball to strike the front wall at a height of about 16 to 18 feet from the floor. The distance from the sidewall is the same as that of the low Z serve. When hit properly, the ball—after traveling cross-court—will bounce and hit the back wall. But, due to the spin on the ball, it will pop directly off the back wall, parallel with the sidewall. If the ball is hit deep enough into the pocket of the corner, it will hug or be so close to the sidewall that a successful return will be very difficult.

THE CROSS-COURT SERVE

The cross-court serve is initiated from the same place as the Z serves. It is actually used as a method of keeping your opponent guessing at your serve selection.

This serve will appear to be a low Z serve. However, it will strike the front wall approximately 10 to 12 inches from centercourt closest to the far sidewall and fly to the back corner. If your opponent anticipates the low Z or is flat-footed just momentarily, the result can be a point for you. You will discover it only takes one time of catching your opponent off balance to make him or her respond to your serve after the ball is in flight.

Experimenting with these serves can be interesting and fun. As you become more familiar with them and have gained confidence in their execution, analyze why they are effective. For example, the Z serve is particularly effective due to the spin the ball acquires from the contact with the front wall-sidewall. Thus, spin can be an effective tool in serving.

You will find that slicing the ball on the lob serve will result in the ball coming off the front wall and bouncing surprisingly close to the sidewall. Be creative in your choice of serves and in the variation of the serves.

COURT POSITION—OFFENSE

After you have served the ball, you should put yourself in a position that is advantageous to play your opponent's return of your serve. This can be done quite easily, but must be decided before contact with the ball has been

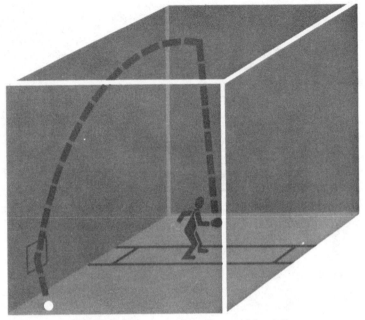

High lob shot touches sidewall on descent into the back court, and doesn't come off the back wall.

made by you. You are the only one who knows where the serve is headed—either to the left or right corner.

First, decide into which corner the ball will be headed. Then, after you make contact with the ball, you will want to position yourself similar to that of a third base coach in a baseball game. Stand about two to three feet behind the service box and one to two feet from the center, closest to the sidewall opposite the path of the ball. You will actually be facing the side-wall. In this way, you will be able to respond to the ball as it leaves your opponent's racquet and you'll be in good court position to set up for the ball if your opponent has not executed a return that forces you out of the center of the court.

COURT POSITION—DEFENSE

In defense against a serve, always position yourself in the middle of the court about three to four feet from the back wall. You should be relaxed but eager to jump on the serve.

Drive serve is made from the middle of service box, and your contact point will be at knee height as you step into the ball.

Stand facing straight ahead with your feet spread apart to shoulder width and bend at the knees, similar to a shortstop in baseball.

COURT PSYCHOLOGY IN SERVES

As you get ready to serve the ball, you should appear motionless. However, much activity should be going on inside your head. Look closely at your opponent. Does he or she appear to be expecting one specific type of serve? Is the opponent standing in the middle of the court? Is the returnee's racquet fixed as though anticipating you hitting to his or her backhand? Is the opponent's feet positioned for one specific corner? Is the returnee frustrated or tired?

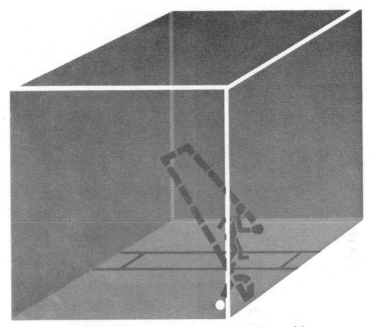

Z serve is hit from a point midway between the sidewall and the center of the court. Ball will strike front wall, bounce to the sidewall and come across the court.

Concentrate on the fundamentals of the serve you have selected. Remind yourself to move into good court position after you have served the ball.

As the game progresses, be aware of how effective your serves have been on your opponent. Notice if your opponent returns one specific type of serve in the same manner. If so, your anticipation of the return can give you the edge to catch the opponent off guard. If a specific serve is difficult for your foe to return, modify it slightly so the opponent does not begin to understand what he or she is doing wrong.

Remember, you have worked hard to get the serve. You now control the momentum of the game. Be confident. It's now your turn to score points. You are on the offense. Play each point as though you only needed one more point to win the match. Keep yourself interested in the result of the selection of your serve. If you tune into the tempo of the match, your opponent's frame of mind, and the score, you can size up what is best suited at the time of each serve. Be aware!

In making a drive serve, drop the ball out in front of you. Do not bounce the ball as you don't need the extra height, your contact point being at knee height.

Getting ready to hit a Z serve. Step to the direction you want the ball to take and concentrate on keeping your eye on the ball.

Hitting a drive serve to opponent's forehand. Note how foot movement steps in line to where you want to hit to front wall.

Note foot positioning at point of contact for same drive serve when you want the ball to go to opponent's backhand.

Cross court serve. Server positions self so that opponent is unaware of type of serve—server can hit Z shot or cross-court pass.

After serving the ball, put yourself in a center-court position that is advantageous to play your opponent's return of your serve.
54

Chapter 6

SHOTS

In racquetball, knowing when to use a shot is just as important as knowing how to execute it. It is not uncommon to find most new players quickly learning a new shot but not knowing when or where to place their shot.

Many beginning and intermediate players will frequently comment that not only do good players make the fundamentals of the game seem easy, but their shots seem to fall in the right place at the right time. Once you have mastered the shots used in racquetball, you will begin to understand how very logical and predictable this game can be played. With a repertoire of shots under control, you can easily pick apart your opponent's game.

Observe a rally between players just getting started and you will notice many forehand shots that are hit low and hard but placed in easy access of the opponent. The shot was well executed but the placement was poor.

Racquetball is unique in that there may be several answers or methods employed in your shot selection en route to victory. Let's take a look at shot techniques and the proper time to use them.

Shots in racquetball can be divided into two groups: those designed to score points and those to provide you the court position to score. There will be opportunities when you will have your opponent at the mercy of your successful execution of your shot, and there will be times when you will need to hit the ball so that your opponent is not put in an advantageous position.

Making contact for a backhand shot. Step into the ball for contact out in front of you.

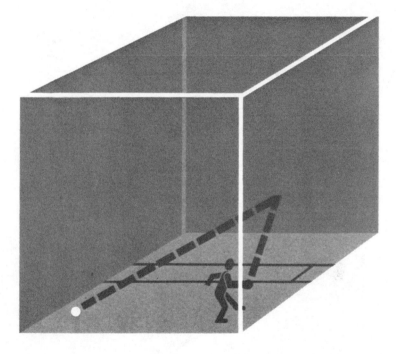

Cross-court pass shot. Shot should strike
the front wall and be angled to either of
the back wall corners.

This is a pass shot that comes straight down along sidewall closest to the hitter and furthest from the opponent.

Player shows proper form, waiting for the ball to reach the correct height for better contact point.

This player, in hitting a ball from the backwall, has reacted emotionally and is out of proper form, unable to swing level and hit at her side.

In teaching racquetball fundamentals, we find it easy to explain by comparing it to strategy used in a game of pool. When you have a clear shot at putting the ball in the pocket, you take it. But when you have no high percentage shot, you try to hit the ball so that after it stops, your opponent will be faced with the same situation.

Whether you use an offensive or defensive shot, be aggressive. If you change your mode of play during a game, you will lose your concentration and ultimately your chance to dominate the game.

Let's first take a look at offensive shots. Picture yourself with an opportunity to score a point or win the serve. Generally, you will know that you are in this position when you are taking your shot from an area not further back than three to four feet from the service line.

THE FRONT WALL SHOT

Making a shot off the front wall is similar in its fundamentals to that of learning the forehand or backhand strokes. Your goal is to get the ball to strike the front wall as low as possible. This can be achieved by making contact with the ball when it is out in front of you at a height of about six to eight inches from the floor.

A low shot comes from bending low, stepping into the ball with your swing parallel to the ground. This shot should be selected when you are in the middle or front of the court and when your opponent is behind you. Beginning players, as well as experienced players, become very nervous when attempting this shot. Do not let your opponent's presence disturb you. Concentrate on the fundamentals involved with the shot and place the shot to the side of the court opposite your opponent.

When you have the opportunity to use this shot, be determined and confident, knowing that a properly hit front-wall shot will not be returned.

THE PINCH SHOT

The pinch shot is one that hits the sidewall first before striking the front wall. It is an especially good shot for beginners to master for several reasons.

First, it can help relieve the pressure of shooting a front wall kill shot. It is an excellent way to become acquainted with understanding the angles of the court. In addition, it can be used from almost any place on the court that you are able to set up and step into the ball.

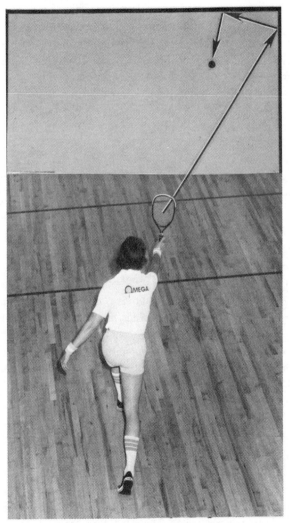

Path of ball in overhead kill shot from the back of the court. Goal is to get ball to strike front wall as low as possible.

The pinch shot can be hit to either wall and should be developed as both a forehand and backhand selection. It is executed in a similar manner as the front-wall shot. However, you need not hit the ball as low as the forehand shot. The ball should be hit at knee level as you step into the ball and hit the sidewall approximately 18 to 24 inches from the front wall.

The ball's flight from sidewall to front wall will bring the shot down very low. Therefore, the pressure the novice player feels in waiting for the low contact point in the forehand is not existent in this shot.

There are only two limitations to when the shot should be selected. First, do not choose the pinch shot when your opponent is in front of you. Secondly, as the ball comes off the front wall, be sure that it will not be in line to bounce toward your opponent. The ball should be hit so that it has bounced on the floor twice before it reaches the first service line.

THE TOUCH SHOT

During the game you will want to vary not only your selection of shots but the speed. The touch shot can be used with the same effectiveness a baseball pitcher utilizes his knuckleball for a change of pace. The touch shot is actually a modification to the front wall or pinch shots. The only difference in the execution of the touch shot is the velocity of the ball. It should be hit in the same manner as the lob serve.

As you step into the ball you will roll your wrist at a reduced quickness. You have put the proper velocity or wrist snap into this shot when the ball strikes the front wall and seems to die as it dribbles away from the wall.

It can be used anytime your opponent is several feet behind you or he is in the rear of the court. Remember not to telegraph the shot by moving or reacting slower than usual. The only noticeable difference in this shot should be in the wrist action. This sudden change-of-pace play will usually catch your opponent flat-footed or reacting to the ball after it has hit the floor twice.

THE PASS SHOT

In the three previous shots, we have said not to select the shot when your opponent is in front of you. The pass shot is designed for use when you are *behind* your opponent. This ball is hit with the same feeling as the drive serve.

The contact point with the ball should be at knee height. The shot should

Male player has made poor shot selection, hitting to front of court when female opponent is in advantageous center-court position.

strike the front wall and be angled to either of the back wall corners. You will know that you have hit this shot properly when you observe your opponent turning, racing to the back wall only too late as the ball bounces twice before hitting the back wall. This shot should always be hit to the corner furthest from your opponent. Therefore, if you are next to a side-wall and your opponent is closer to the opposite wall, you will want to shoot the ball so that it comes back to the corner closest to you. When the ball takes this path, it often is referred to as a shot that travels down the wall.

THE OVERHEAD KILL

An overhead kill is a shot that can be used very effectively but is not often selected by those new to the sport. It is an important shot to learn. You must be aware of its difficulty in execution.

What actually makes this shot difficult is its unique method of combining the contact point of the ball with its desired path. The stroke form is similar to that of throwing a baseball. Your arm motion should be parallel to your body. Be aware of the difference in this motion as compared to the other shots. The contact point of the ball will be out in front of you and it should be on an imaginary line beginning about two inches above your shoulder and ending at the sidewall approximately six inches from the front wall and about 12 inches from the floor. It should only be used when you and your opponent are in the back court.

The overhead kill is most frequently used in the return of a ceiling shot. Once you've learned the ceiling shot you will understand why.

OFF-THE-BACK-WALL SHOT

Playing the ball as it comes off the back wall can seem confusing. The inexperienced players usually seem to be chasing the ball, rather than being set up for the ball.

You always want to react to the ball, not after the ball. Actually, learning to control a back wall shot can be easy. This play can be easily executed by learning to anticipate the bounce the ball will take as it comes off the back wall.

There are two types of off-the-back-wall shots. After the ball has hit the front wall, it can either hit the floor before it reaches the back wall or hit the back wall on a fly. The key to playing these shots is positioning. As soon as you realize the path of the ball, react immediately. If the ball strikes the floor, position yourself four to five feet from the back wall. If the ball is going to hit the back wall without bouncing you will be positioned about seven to eight feet from the ball. Then, as the ball comes off the wall, move with the direction of the ball so that you can hit the ball at its proper contact point.

We have not stated the height of the contact point, simply because it may vary with your shot selection.

Probably the most difficult thing in learning this shot will be to move forward in the court as you see the ball go past you. Most players will catch themselves moving to the direction of the ball. If you have positioned yourself properly, and in line with the ball, you will soon notice that most times the ball comes off the back wall, you will be able to score a point or win the serve. The reason for this is quite simple: as you wait for the ball, you will have a good indication of where your opponent has positioned himself.

DEFENSIVE SHOTS

Defensive shots used in racquetball must not be treated in a passive mood. Basically, these shots are designed to deny your opponent the opportunity to score on the next shot when you are taking a shot out of good court position.

If you do not have a proper setup to score on your shot, you will want your opponent to be in the same situation when it's his or her turn to hit the ball.

It's not uncommon to find more experienced players becoming involved in a defensive rally with each competitor waiting for the other to hit the ball poorly and provide a chance to score. Although these shots are defensive, if they are properly placed they can be so difficult to return that they will result in a point. Therefore, think of them only as defensive in the sense that you cannot score on a kill shot, but offensive in that they may be unsuccessfully returned or provide you with the court position to score on your next shot.

THE CEILING BALL

The ceiling ball is the most commonly used defensive shot and probably one of the most popular shots in racquetball. Perhaps the reason for its appeal among beginners is the fact that you soon become aware you are hitting a shot which reflects a certain degree of knowledge about the sport. Moreover, it is interesting to watch the play of the ball after it has bounced from the front wall.

The form for this shot is similar to that we described in the overhead kill shot. You should step into the ball with an overhead stroke. The arm motion resembles that of throwing a baseball. As you bring your arm past your ear, it begins to straighten and as contact is made with the ball, you will snap your wrist forward. Your contact point with the ball should be approximately eight inches above your shoulder and in line with the face of your racquet and a spot on the ceiling about 10 to 12 inches from the front wall.

For a backhand ceiling shot you will need to modify your form due to the fact that the backhand shot would cause you to lose your balance if hit in an overhand manner. The backhand shot should be hit about four to five inches away from the body. Angle your ceiling shot so that it bounces to either of the corners. Note that we did not say the corner opposite your opponent. If your foe is in the backhand corner, you may decide that you still want him or her to play the ball to their backhand.

You will know that you have executed this shot properly when it hits the ceiling and front wall, bounces down to the floor and takes a high arc—one which carries the ball high and into the corner and dies as it hits the back wall.

This shot can be used anywhere in the court when you are not in position to take an offensive shot. It is similar to the tennis lob.

As you become more confident in your ability to use this shot effectively, your placement of the ball will become easy.

THE Z SHOT

One of the most valuable shots to have at your command is the Z shot. It's not seen often by new players because it's more difficult.

At times you may find yourself in the front court position and unclear as to which shot to select. Your uncertainty may come from not clearly knowing the court position of your opponent.

The Z shot will drive your opponent into the back court. If your foe is too late to anticipate the path of the ball, the opponent may be unsuccessful in returning your shot.

The Z shot is similar to the Z serve, with one major exception. It should be hit with sufficient power to carry the ball from the front wall to the

Player has just made contact with a ceiling ball, hitting from a backhand. Angle the shot so it bounces to either of the corners.

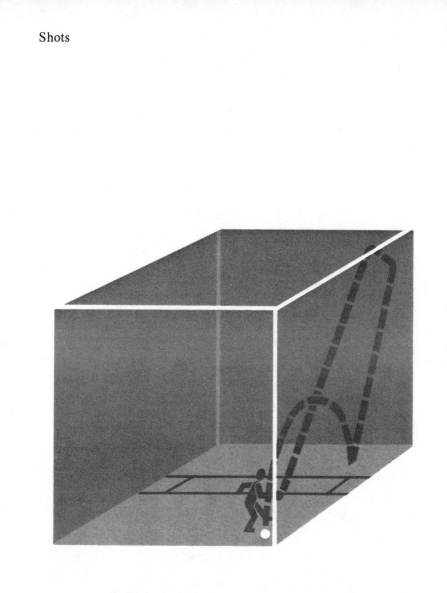

Ceiling shot is properly executed when it hits the ceiling and front wall, bounces down to the floor and takes a high arc, carrying the ball into the corner and dying as it hits the back wall.

opposite side wall on a fly. Due to the spin of the ball—resulting from the sidewall to front wall hit—the ball will bounce off the sidewall parallel with the back wall. After you have hit this shot, don't become engulfed with its pattern of flight. Move into good court position. Remember the concept of the ball's flight pattern is the Z shot. This will be especially helpful to you as you position yourself to await your opponent's return. Use a quick wrist snap as you execute this shot as it will result in greater spin and sufficient power.

THE BACK WALL SHOT

This shot is only to be used in time of desperation. The ball has come off the front wall and you are unable to set up for a return. At this moment, you will hit the ball into the back wall, which will carry it on a fly to the front wall. Use this shot when it is the only shot that can keep the rally going. Because you cannot accurately place the ball, it's a last-resort shot.

Observe carefully as you begin to learn this shot. It's not uncommon for a beginner to hit the ball into the wall and have it come directly back at him. Inexperienced players have been known to hit their racquet into the back wall and have their own racquet bounce back and strike them in the head.

Due to the nature of this shot, your only considerations should be to hit the ball at an angle away from your body and to place the ball high enough on the back wall so that it will carry to the front wall on a fly.

Those are the various shots commonly used in racquetball. Do not make the mistake of becoming so engrossed with the technique of the shot that you are unaware of the proper time to use it. Use a particular shot only when it seems logical—that, if done properly, it will score a point or help keep your opponent from scoring.

Ceiling shot is made overhand, similar to a baseball throw. Player has made contact and is beginning follow through.

Professionals and advanced players learn to make contact at ankle height in executing a front wall kill shot. Taller player needs to bend more to reach ball.

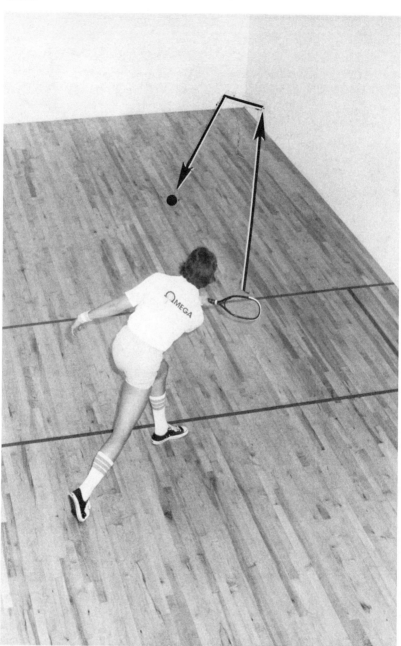

Pinch shot is used when you are in the center of the court and your opponent to the rear. Ball goes to front of court, far from foe.

Player is in position for anticipation of a shot requiring a backhand return.

Player is shown following through after hitting a front wall pinch shot. Note how feet are positioned toward sidewall.

In hitting a ceiling ball, the contact point is approximately eight inches above your shoulder. Snap wrist forward on contact.

When hitting a backwall-to-front wall shot, hit the ball away from your body to avoid being hit by your own shot.

Player in foreground, unaware of opponent's position, selected a Z shot to drive foe to back court so that he can move into advantageous center-court position.

Chapter 7

DEFENSIVE PLAY:
FOOTWORK AND CONCENTRATION

In the preceding chapters we concentrated on offensive play. In this chapter we shall delve into the important aspects of defensive play.

Defensive play involves two basic categories: 1) how should you react as you await the ball and 2) what thoughts should be going through your mind.

Let's examine the physical factor in defensive play, namely footwork. The primary goal of footwork in racquetball should be to place you in a position where you will be able to stroke the ball properly. Obviously, there will be times when the location of the ball will not enable you to set up for the "step-into" technique of strokes. However, in these instances, if you have used the proper footwork in getting to the ball, your chances of a successful return will be greatly improved.

Proper footwork on the court can be as important to a racquetball player as it can be to a boxer in a ring. Proper footwork not only means getting to the ball, but reaching the spot on the court while placing yourself in the correct position to stroke the ball effectively and in an aggressive manner.

Does it seem paradoxical to be concerned with aggressive play when we talk about defensive action? Well, you must be aggressive throughout your game. Defensive play is actually a modification of your offensive action. Once you think of yourself as playing a defensive game you will be subjecting yourself to follow the momentum and lead of your opponent.

As you await your opponent's serve, you should be positioned similar to a shortstop in baseball. Your legs should be spread apart approximately four to six inches beyond shoulder width. Your upper body should be bent slightly so that your wrists could rest lightly on your knees. Your head should be straight forward and you should be standing on the balls of your feet. From this ready position you are prepared to move either to the right or left in response to the path of the ball.

There are three basic foot movements utilized in covering the court. Probably the most natural movement comes from moving toward the ball when it's hit in front of you. When this occurs you should move to the ball with the same motion as running. Just before you reach the ball, turn to the side for the step-in technique. Whenever you must move back into the court to pursue a ball, your movement should be like that of a wide receiver in football who is running a pattern and looking for the pass. Your movement is in the manner of a run and you should be constantly looking over your shoulder to keep continual eye contact with the ball. You can set up for the shot when you are able to anticipate the path of the ball.

The most common movement on the court is from side to side. Anytime you must move laterally, your feet will move in a shuffle manner. This shuffling pattern can best be described as a side step movement, similar to a waltz-type dance step. The side-to-side movement should not be limited to lateral positioning. This type of footwork should be utilized whenever possible. Thus, if the position of the ball requires a movement of three to four feet in front or behind you, this shuffle movement is very useful. The sooner you are in proper position to make contact with the ball, the better your chance to execute a good shot. A side-to-side movement allows you to arrive at the ball in position to make contact without requiring you to shift your stance due to the quickness of the game. A lost second can be enough time to cause you to hit the ball from an improper position and poor form.

COURT ANTICIPATION

Probably one of the most difficult decisions for the novice and intermediate player is where to place the ball. During a rally, the player becomes involved in the excitement of a quickly-paced match. It is during this time of your development that you must begin to emphasize logic rather than emotion in your game.

It's easy to recognize players involved in an emotional rally. The ball may be hit with proper form, but each player seems to be in the correct place to return the opponent's shot.

With her opponent out in front and to the side of her, player at rear goes for a cross-court pass shot.

All play in racquetball must be based on logic. Inexperienced players will ask: "How can I have the time to think of playing a game solely based on logic when the ball moves so fast and I barely have time to set up properly for a shot?"

We've developed a technique to help players understand where to logically place the ball. It's essential to understand that defense in racquetball is simply based on where your shot has been placed on the court. There are times when you must shoot the ball to score a point and there are times when you must try to hit the ball in such a way to keep your opponent from getting into court position to score a point against you.

In understanding our method of court anticipation, imagine that the court is divided into four equal squares: front right, rear right, front left and rear left. Whenever you can clearly identify your opponent's location, see which quarter of the court he or she is occupying. When you've determined the location, stroke the ball so that after hitting the front wall, it will carry to the quarter of the court directly opposite your opponent's location. There's no guarantee that this form of logical play will win a point in each rally. But if the ball is placed properly after your opponent has returned your shot, he or she may be so out of position as to leave you with an easy set-up on your next shot.

The only time you may decide to alter this type of strategy may come from the confidence that you can kill the ball. However, this type of confidence will only be attained after you have thoroughly mastered this type of four-square court logic.

If you are involved in a rally when you are unable to identify the location of your opponent, the ceiling ball or Z shot may prove to be very valuable. As your opponent is driven to the back court to return your shot, you can move into the center of the court and await the action. Never make a shot that will result in the ball coming off the wall and occupying the same square as your opponent.

If your opponent has left you in a situation in which you cannot clearly make a logical shot, select a shot which will leave him or her in a situation to make a low percentage shot—that is, one in which the shot is taken from an awkward stance or the ball, after striking the front wall, carries to the opposite square not occupied by your opponent.

Utilizing this four-square logic will allow you more time to set up properly to return your opponent's shot. As soon as the ball strikes the front wall, decide which quarter of the court the ball will carry to and move toward that location. Learn to form a habit of reacting at the moment the

Overhead kill shot should only be used when you and your opponent are in the back court. It's frequently used to return a ceiling shot.

When ball carries to backwall on a fly after bouncing on floor, position yourself three to five feet from backwall; if ball hits front wall and carries to backwall on fly, your position should be seven to eight feet from the backwall.

Positioning yourself on defense like a shortstop in a baseball game enables you to move quickly to your left or right.

Player on right shows poor positioning as he is standing too erect to react quickly to opponent's shot.

Player is making a lateral movement as she prepares for a forehand shot. Try to make contact at waist height if you're a beginner.

This player is set up with her racquet back in anticipation of making a backhand shot. She will step into ball as she hits it.

ball hits the front wall. Inexperienced players tend to react after the ball has carried 10 to 12 feet away from the front wall.

It's interesting to note that as you become trained to key on the ball you will be able to accurately predict the eventual location of the ball sometime between the ball's point of contact with your opponent's racquet and the ball's flight before it actually strikes the front wall.

In examining the mental side of racquetball, you should keep in mind that once the ball has been served, you are on equal ground with your opponent and you should be just as aggressive as on offense.

It is very common to hear players note that their match seemed to fall apart or lose some of its intensity after the first game. This is due to lack of mental endurance—not maintaining full concentration. Each shot you make should be based on logic, not emotion. After each rally, analyze briefly what transpired. If necessary, call time out and think about your positioning and shot selection. It is vital that you learn why you are effective or ineffective. Train yourself to continually analyze your game. Play each point with the intensity as if it were the last point needed to win the match. You will soon become aware that the more you mentally push yourself, the more logical, effective and enjoyable your game will develop.

Mental endurance does not come easy, but when noticeably increased the benefits to your play are greatly enhanced. Note we have mentioned enjoyment as one of the benefits of a logical game. Any activity which allows you to understand the effectiveness of your actions will become increasingly more pleasurable. If you are unable to win, you will at least understand why. And to most recreation players, while winning may not be important, a comprehension of the essence of the game is very rewarding.

Mental errors will generally prove to be more detrimental than the physical mistakes. An error in technique can be noticed and corrected in a relatively short time. But unless you analyze your movements on the court, you may spend many hours trying to understand why you seem to react to the ball, rather than why you are not controlling the momentum of the game.

At this point, in the development of your game, it will be beneficial to spend some time watching different matches. It's not important to observe games between experienced players as they will not be the focal point of your attention. Watch only the action of the ball. Learn to understand the path the ball will take after striking a different combination of walls at different speeds and heights. You will soon become aware that your game will noticeably improve as you begin to anticipate the flight of the ball after

Lateral movements to the right and left are frequently required in racquetball. Good footwork is vital for defensive skills.

it has left the front wall.

If you will carefully observe different games, you will find it very satisfying to position yourself on the court, observe the ball hitting three walls and bounce to the location where you are awaiting to make contact with the ball.

Player moves to back court in pursuit of ball. He keeps his eye on the ball similar to football player out for a pass.

Player is already in position and using proper form for stepping into the ball.

Here a ceiling ball is hit from the rear of the court as opponent moves back to the rear of court to make contact with ball. Hitter then moves to advantageous center court position to await return of ball.

Chapter 8

DOUBLES PLAY AND HINDERS

Doubles play is becoming increasingly popular in racquetball. Thus, newcomers to the sport should learn the basic fundamentals of playing doubles for added enjoyment.

Two important factors enter into doubles play: 1) hinders, which involves blocking or interfering with your opponent's fair chance to see and return the ball and 2) safety, which means being able to play free from worry of being injured.

At many racquetball clubs, organized doubles play is an important part of the program and they only allow experienced players to participate on this level. There are several levels of organized singles play but for members' safety, many clubs are very restrictive about who may be involved in doubles competition.

Because the size of the court does not increase when you play doubles, it is essential that you and your partner have a clear understanding of team strategy and positioning. First, you and your partner must be knowledgeable of each other's strengths and weaknesses. Establishing a strong rapport with your partner is vital for success. Many doubles matches are won by a team composed of weaker individual players who are well united in their team strategy.

In deciding court position, the player with the stronger backhand should play on the left side because, as with singles, the backhand side usually receives the brunt of your opponents' attack.

Any shot that comes down the middle of the court should be taken by the player on the left because it allows that player to hit the ball with his forehand. This is beneficial to your team not only due to the forehand use but the fact that the stronger backhand player is usually the more proficient player.

It is not uncommon for doubles teams to be formed with a righthanded and lefthanded player. The premise behind this formation is that the average player is stronger and more effective with the forehand than the backhand. Therefore, two forehands on the same team provide that side an added dimension of strength.

Do not think of doubles play as meaning that each player is responsible only for his or her half or side of the court. The most effective form of play is what is called the "revolving" method. As a player moves out of his or her initial court position, the partner helps cover the area vacated by moving into the center of the court. Both players continue to occupy their positions until they are able to resume their original position of court coverage.

If a rally forces a player to return the ball from the side opposite his or her original position, the player continues to be responsible for that side of the court. The partner, likewise, then assumes his or her new side. The idea behind this play is to continually have your team maximize complete flexibility of coverage as you rotate into court position. In other words, when your partner is moved out of an original position on the court, the partner will be assuming the responsibility of part of your court coverage. You, in return, must cover that portion of the court that your partner can no longer defend. Thus, each partner continues to defend half of the court, but the boundaries of that half may change several times during a rally. When you and your partner have achieved this type of movement, your team will be in complete harmony. Each player will have a good understanding of where the other is positioned on the court and you will both feel actively involved in the action.

While involved in the action you and your partner should shout words of encouragement to each other during a rally. As a team you should try to bring out the best play in each other. Do not hesitate to call for a time-out to discuss or analyze what is happening to your match. You may have noticed something that your partner hasn't observed.

Many times a player may interfere with an opponent's attempt to hit the ball. Most of the times this is due to the player's lack of knowledge about where to position one's self after hitting the ball. It is very important to avoid hindering your opponent—not only because you are interrupting

Ready to serve in a doubles match. Partner is in service box. Opponents divide back court, each standing three to five feet from backwall.

Male player at rear has just hit ball to right corner; woman moves close to wall (this page). Next shot went to opposite corner. Woman moved to right side and partner switched to left side (next page).

play but to avoid injury to yourself and/or your opponent. Such interference may occur only occasionally in a singles match, but may be quite frequent in doubles play due to the number of players and the restrictive boundaries of the court.

Anytime a player is denied the opportunity to see and return the ball, it is a hindrance. You must give your opponent a clear path to return your shot. You must not obstruct the player in any manner. Moreover, while you await your opponent's shot, you may not crowd the player so as to interfere with the follow-through of the swing.

Most hinders will usually be played over during a game. However, if a player continually or purposely hinders the opponent, the opponent may be awarded a point.

Hinders come generally under two categories: intentional or unintentional.

Beginning players quite often will unintentionally block or screen off their opponent's view of the ball. This is usually due to the result of not being aware of where the ball is going. The best way to remedy this situation is through proper shot selection. Be aware of where your opponent will have to move in order to return your shot, then position yourself so that you will be able to observe the player and react immediately to the return.

When players place more emphasis on winning than in playing to the best of their ability, it is not uncommon for them to intentionally block or deny their opponent a fair chance to see and return the ball. This kind of an attitude is extremely detrimental to the game. It ruins any degree of pleasure which could be attained during the match and increases the chance for injury. Our best advice to this type of player is to simply rely upon the confidence in his or her own ability.

If you find yourself playing someone who intentionally hinders you, walk off the court and find somebody else to play. You will eliminate the chance of injury to yourself and, hopefully, cause your opponent to think about why you have prematurely ended the match. Anytime your opponent intentionally hinders you during a tournament match, the opponent will be penalized by the official, who will award you with a point.

The most common area for dispute in racquetball comes from calling a hinder. There are times when calling a hinder is a matter of judgment. While you may feel that you have positioned yourself out of the direct line of action, your opponent may believe a fair chance was denied to return the ball. When this occurs, good sportsmanship can be the only solution. Show

This is considered a hinder as the player on left is preparing to hit a shot, but his opponent is interfering with his follow through.

Player in foreground turned back to opponent and positioned self in front of him, blocking his shot. This is a hinder.

A hinder is called when a player stands in the way of his opponent's follow through of a shot.

Imagine the court in four equal squares. Player hitting ball in front court has selected a pinch shot to keep ball in front-right court because opponent is occupying back left quadrant of court.

your opponent respect and allow the rally to be played over. In this way you will be setting the precedence for your opponent's actions in the event that you think you have been hindered.

During a match, you may find that your follow-through in your swing will make contact with your opponent. When this occurs, simply call a hinder and allow the rally to be repeated. Your opponent will become aware of the emphasis you have placed on playing a safe, non-hazardous game.

It's a good idea to always place emphasis in playing a safe game to the fullest extent of your ability. Rely solely upon your ability and strategy to win. If you have achieved a good workout and had an enjoyable game, you shall have found satisfaction. Winning, although important, is secondary.

At any club, the players who are regarded as enjoyable to play with are almost always those who emphasize fairness and safety, and not solely proficiency of the game.

With ball coming down the middle of court, opponent on right side gives partner on left chance to hit ball, thus allowing partner to play ball with forehand.

Chapter 9

DRILLS, STRATEGY, TOURNAMENTS

Once you have learned the basic fundamentals of playing racquetball and become a better player, you may want to consider competing in tournamants. Tournament play can increase your enjoyment of the sport, so it's definitely something to think about.

Whether you aspire to play in tournaments or not, practice should become a regular part of your schedule if you want to continue to improve and further enhance the pleasures of the sport.

Players who avoid practice generally do so because they find it's tedious. Practice can be done without boredom if you fully concentrate on further development of new techniques. In practice, you are not under any form of pressure. Therefore, you can concentrate solely on sound fundamentals while free from any distractions. You can develop your skills more thoroughly during practice than you can while involved in a match. Techniques developed during practice will form your playing habits in match play.

Our advice is that you practice the basic fundamental shots as we have described them in the aforegoing chapters. You can also be more imaginative in your practice sessions by tossing a ball to different spots in the court and at different heights and by throwing the ball against a sidewall, back wall or combination of walls.

You can vary your practice period by combining two different types of shots in your drills. For example, hit a ceiling ball from the back of the court; as the ball returns to the back court, step into the ball and hit an over-head kill shot.

As you practice this form of drill, imagine yourself involved in actual play. Therefore, be patient and deliberate. You can throw the ball to the back wall. As it comes off the back wall, imagine that your opponent has stayed in the back court, and thus select a pinch shot. Try this again, but as the ball comes off the back wall, imagine that your opponent has charged to the front of the court in anticipation of a pinch shot. Therefore, select a pass shot down the wall opposite your opponent.

Be creative in your shot selection, but remember to combine only those shots which will logically fit into your game.

If it is difficult for you to master a certain fundamental, it may be helpful to practice your body movements in front of a mirror, or to have a friend observe you in action.

How long should you practice? The time you spend on practice depends upon how quick you are able to learn a specific technique and on what level of play you wish to aspire. Of course, the best indicator of how long to practice will probably come from the level of enjoyment you attain on the court. If you are happy with your level of skill, you will probably spend little time practicing. But if you seek to improve your game, practice will become more important to you.

STRATEGY

Perhaps the most difficult task for the racquetball player, whether on the beginning or intermediate level, is to combine all of the components of the game into a logical semblance of order. Actually, the basic philosophy of this game is very comprehendable. Usually, the player who is able to hit the ball from the center court position will emerge victorious. When you occupy the center of the court, your opponent must position himself or herself around you. If the opponent is in the back court, you can score on a shot designed to keep the ball in the front court. If the opponent charges to the front court, select a shot that will place the ball in the back court. If your opponent should position himself or herself in center court, but on your side, select a pass shot along the wall to the opposite side.

Should you find yourself out of center court, select a defensive shot which will drive your opponent out of the center and into the right or left back corner. As your opponent moves after the shot, move to center court. If your opponent's shot does not drive you from center court, you now are

A good practice drill is hitting repeated ceiling balls, one of the most commonly used defensive shots.

in excellent position to score.

Do not react emotionally to the play of the ball, but interpret the mode of the game and select logical shots. Many players become nervous and find it difficult to keep their composure as they wait for the ball to arrive at the proper height for contact with their racquet. This uneasiness stems from being aware of your opponent who is trying to anticipate where you will shoot the ball. The key to avoiding this uneasiness is to understand that it is to your advantage to wait for the ball to make proper contact. Not only will waiting allow you to hit the ball fluidly with correct form but will force your opponent to position himself or herself.

As you become aware of your opponent's court position, you will then be able to select a shot designed to place the ball in a location away from your opponent and win yourself a point.

As you become more proficient at using the basic fundamentals, you should begin to develop the ability to analyze the style and effectiveness of your own performance and that of your opponent. This is where strategy enters the picture. Strategy is your own plan to achieve victory. It is based on maximizing your strengths and exposing your opponent's weaknesses. Each opponent you face has different strengths and weaknesses and your own performance may vary on a specific day. Therefore, your strategy can never be fixed.

There are times when you will want to modify your strategy during a match. This can occur when you discover your opponent is stronger than you anticipated or if your own performance is not up to par. By calling a time out, you can pause to analyze what is happening on the court. Unless you have already observed your opponent, you may have to develop your strategy as the game is played. Formulating your plan of attack during the match is not as difficult as it sounds.

Concentrate on three areas of your opponent's play. First, as you begin play, watch how your opponent moves on the court. Observe the player to see whether he or she can hit the ball effectively while moving laterally. Observe your opponent's position on the court after the player has hit the ball.

Practice throwing the ball to the backwall and stepping into the ball as it rebounds off the wall.

Secondly, use a wide variety of shots against your opponent. This will enable you to become aware of the player's strengths and weaknesses. You will learn that one type of shot will be more effective than another. Using this knowledge, try to control the momentum of the game by hitting shots that could result in weak returns.

Third, try to interpret your opponent's plan of attack. Observe the pattern of play. Note whether a specific type of shot is selected for certain plays. For example, does the player prefer to try a kill shot from the back court rather than hitting a ceiling ball?

Only when you fully understand your opponent's strategy will you be able to anticipate the player's movements and shot selections.

Naturally, the best time to search for your opponent's weaknesses and strengths and to learn the player's plan of attack is in the very beginning of play. Be very observant from the very first serve. You must also be aggressive.

TOURNAMENTS

Participation in racquetball tournaments is offered to players on all levels of performance—from novice to professional. Tournaments can be open to competitors throughout the country or limited to the membership in a specific racquetball club.

Participation in a tournament can be a very rewarding experience. Considerable personal satisfaction can be achieved. In some clubs, tournaments also include buffets, exhibition matches, and souvenirs. Friends and families of members are encouraged to attend as spectators. The emphasis is placed on having a good time in a healthful atmosphere. The spirit of competition, good sportsmanship, meeting new friends, and playing against a variety of players all combine to make it an interesting experience.

Entering your first tournament may find you a bit nervous, and that's why it's probably best to play your initial tournament at the novice level.

No player should compete in a tournament without a good warmup session. Allow plenty of time for your meals and travel so that you arrive early enough to spend some practice time on the court.

OFFICIATING

As a comparatively new sport, racquetball does not have a list of officials it can readily call upon to referee amateur tournaments. So don't be surprised if you are called upon to officiate a match during a tournament. The thought may at first strike you as an awkward experience, but once you've made up your mind to try, you'll probably find it an enjoyable event. A competent tournament director will not ask you to referee a match between players who are in a higher playing division than yourself.

After introducing yourself to the players, toss a coin to determine who will serve first. Ask the players to please aid you in calling skip shots or double bounces. However, remind them that you will be responsible for all calls and that your decision is final. Before each serve, call out the score. Announce the server's score first, and be sure that both players can hear you. Keep several towels on hand for the players' use during their time outs, or if needed to wipe the floor of the court.

Do not presume anything and never ask for the opinion of scorers or spectators. Due to the limitation of the court's visibility, it is the player's responsibility to correct a call that has been mistakenly awarded in his or her favor. The referee calls all hinders. However, if a player does not swing at the ball and states that was done for safety reasons, a hinder may be called. Do no be hesitant about calling an avoidable hinder, as it could mean eliminating a possible injury.

Explain to both players that there will be no warnings. Be decisive in your judgments.

When you have completed officiating a match, you will discover that you have added another dimension to your own enjoyment of racquetball.

A good drill is throwing the ball to the sidewall so it hits the backwall and carries to the corner enabling you to learn to react to the ball when it hits two walls.

In this practice drill, she hits a ceiling ball, and as the ball comes back from front wall and takes a high arc, she combines another shot—the overhead kill.

Chapter 10

OFFICIAL RACQUETBALL RULES OF THE UNITED STATES RACQUETBALL ASSOCIATION (U.S.R.A.) AND NATIONAL RACQUETBALL CLUB

FOUR-WALL RULES

Part I. The Game

Rule 1.1—Types of Games. Racquetball may be played by two or four players. When played by two it is called "singles"; and when played by four, "doubles."

Rule 1.2—Description. Racquetball, as the name implies, is a competitive game in which a racquet is used to serve and return the ball.

Rule 1.3—Objective. The objective is to win each volley by serving or returning the ball so the opponent is unable to keep the ball in play. A serve or volley is won when a side is unable to return the ball before it touches the floor twice.

Rule 1.4—Points and Outs. Points are scored only by the serving side when it serves an ace or wins a volley. When the serving side loses a volley it loses the serve. Losing the serve is called a "hand-out."

Rule 1.5—Game. A game is won by the side first scoring 21 points.

Rule 1.6—Match. A match is won by the side first winning two games.

Part II. Court and Equipment

Rule 2.1—Court. The specifications for the standard four-wall racquetball court are:

(a) Dimension. The dimensions shall be 20 feet wide, 20 feet high, and 40 feet long, with back wall at least 12 feet high.

(b) Lines and Zones. Racquetball courts shall be divided and marked on the floors with 1½-inch-wide red or white lines as follows:

(1) Short Line. The short line is midway between and is parallel with the front and back walls dividing the court into equal front and back courts.

(2) Service Line. The service line is parallel with and located 5 feet in front of the short line.

(3) Service Zone. The service zone is the space between the outer edges of the short and service lines.

(4) Service Boxes. A service box is located at each end of the service zone by lines 18 inches from and parallel with each side wall.

(5) Receiving Lines. Five feet back of the short line, vertical lines shall be marked on each side wall extending 3 inches from the floor. See rule 4.7(a).

Rule 2.2—Ball Specifications. The specifications for the standard racquetball are:

(a) Official Ball. The official ball of the U.S.R.A. is the black Seamco 558; the official ball of the N.R.C. is the green Seamco 559; or any other racquetball deemed official by the U.S.R.A. or N.R.C. from time to time. The ball shall be 2¼ inches in diameter; weight approximately 1.40 ounces with the bounce at 68-72 inches from 100-inch drop at a temperature of 76 degrees F.

Rule 2.3—Ball Selection. A new ball shall be selected by the referee for use in each match in all tournaments. During a game the referee may, at his discretion or at the request of both players or teams, select another ball. Balls that are not round or which bounce erratically shall not be used.

Rule 2.4—Racquet. The official racquet will have a maximum head length of 11 inches and a width of 9 inches. These measurements are computed from the outer edge of the racquet head rims. The handle may not exceed 7 inches in length. Total length and width of the racquet may not exceed a total of 27 inches.

(a) The racquet must include a thong which must be securely wrapped on the player's wrist.

(b) The racquet frame may be made of any material, as long as it conforms to the above specifications.

(c) The strings of the racquet may be gut, monofilament, nylon, or metal.

Rule 2.5—Uniform. All parts of the uniform, consisting of shirt, shorts and socks, shall be clean, white or of bright colors. Warm-up pants and shirts, if worn in actual match play, shall also be white or of bright colors, but may be of any color if not used in match play. Only club insignia, name of club, name of racquetball organization, name of tournament, or name of sponsor may be on the uniform. Players may not play without shirts.

Part III. Officiating

Rule 3.1—Tournaments. All tournaments shall be managed by a committee or chairman, who shall designate the officials.

Rule 3.2—Officials. The officials shall include a referee and a scorer. Additional assistants and record keepers may be designated as desired.

Rule 3.3—Qualifications. Since the quality of the officiating often determines the success of each tournament, all officials shall be experienced or trained, and shall be thoroughly familiar with these rules and with the local playing conditions.

Rule 3.4—Rule Briefing. Before all tournaments, all officials and players shall be briefed on rules and on local court hinders or other regulations.

Rule 3.5—Referees. (a) Pre-Match Duties. Before each match commences, it shall be the duty of the referee to:

(1) Check on adequacy of preparation of the court with respect to cleanliness, lighting and temperature, and upon location of locker rooms, drinking fountains, etc.

(2) Check on availability and suitability of all materials necessary for the match, such as balls, towels, score cards, and pencils.

(3) Check readiness and qualifications of assisting officials.

(4) Explain court regulations to players and inspect the compliance of racquets with rules.

(5) Remind players to have an adequate supply of extra racquets and uniforms.

(6) Introduce players, toss coin, and signal start of first game.

(b) **Decisions.** During games the referee shall decide all questions that may arise in accordance with these rules. If there is body contact on the back swing, the player should call it quickly. This is the only call a player may make. On all questions involving judgment and on all questions not covered by these rules, the decision of the referee is final.

(c) **Protests.** Any decision not involving the judgment of the referee may on protest be decided by the chairman, if present, or his delegated representative.

(d) **Forfeitures.** A match may be forfeited by the referee when:

(1) Any player refuses to abide by the referee's decision, or engages in unsportsmanlike conduct.

(2) After warning any player leaves the court without permission of the referee during a game.

(3) Any player for a singles match, or any team for a doubles match, fails to report to play. Normally, 20 minutes from the scheduled game time will be allowed before forfeiture. The tournament chairman may permit a longer delay if circumstances warrant such a decision.

(4) If both players for a singles, or both teams for doubles, fail to appear to play for consolation matches or other play-offs, they shall forfeit their ratings for future tournaments, and forfeit any trophies, medals, awards, or prize money.

Rule 3.5 (e) Referee's Technical. The referee is empowered, after giving due warning, to deduct one point from a contestant's or his

team's total score when in the referee's sole judgment, the contestant during the course of the match is being overtly and deliberately abusive beyond a point of reason. The warning referred to will be called a **"Technical Warning"** and the actual invoking of this penalty is called a **"Referee's Technical."** If, after the technical is called against the abusing contestant and the play is not immediately continued within the allotted time provided for under the existing rules, the referee is empowered to forfeit the match in favor of the abusing contestant's opponent or opponents, as the case may be. The **"Referee's Technical"** can be invoked by the referee as many times during the course of a match as he deems necessary.

Rule 3.6—Scorers. The scorer shall keep a record of the progress of the game in the manner prescribed by the committee or chairman. As a minimum the progress record shall include the order of serves, outs, and points. The referee or scorer shall announce the score before each serve.

Rule 3.7—Record Keepers. In addition to the scorer, the committee may designate additional persons to keep more detailed records for statistical purposes of the progress of the game.

Rule 3.8—Linesmen. In any U.S.R.A. or N.R.C. sanctioned tournament match, linesmen may be designated in order to help decide appealed rulings. Two linesmen will be designated by the tournament chairman, and shall at the referee's signal either agree or disagree with the referee's ruling.

The official signal by a linesman to show agreement with the referee is "thumbs up." The official signal to show disagreement is "thumbs down." The official signal for no opinion is an "open palm down."

Both linesmen must disagree with the referee in order to reverse his ruling. If one linesman agrees and one linesman disagrees or has no opinion the referee's call shall stand.

Rule 3.9—Appeals. In any U.S.R.A. or N.R.C. sanctioned tournament match using linesmen, a player or team may appeal certain calls by the referee. These calls are (1) kill shots (whether good or bad); (2) short serves; and (3) double-bounce pick-ups. At no time may a player or team appeal hinder, avoidable hinder, or technical foul calls.

The appeal must be directed to the referee, who will then request opinions from the linesmen. Any appeal made directly to a linesman by a player or team will be considered null and void, and forfeit any appeal rights for that player or team for that particular rally.

(a) Kill Shot Appeals. If the referee makes a call of "good" on a kill shot attempt which ends a particular rally, the loser of the rally may appeal the call, if he feels the shot was not good. If the appeal is successful and the referee's original call reversed, the player who originally lost the rally is declared winner of the rally and is entitled to every benefit under the rules as such, i.e., point and/or service.

If the referee makes a call of "bad" or "skip" on a kill shot attempt, he has ended the rally. The player against whom the call went has the right to appeal the call, if he feels the shot was good. If the appeal is successful and the referee's original call reversed, the player who originally lost the rally is declared winner of the rally and is entitled to every benefit under the rules as winner of a rally.

(b) Short Serve Appeals. If the referee makes a call of "short" on a serve that the server felt was good, the server may appeal the call. If his appeal is successful, the server is then entitled to two additional serves.

If the served ball was considered by the referee to be an ACE serve to the crotch of the floor and side wall and in his opinion there was absolutely no way for the receiver to return the serve, then a point shall be awarded to the server.

If the referee makes a "no call" on a particular serve (therefore making it a legal serve) but either player feels the serve was short, either player may appeal the call at the end of the rally. If the loser of the rally appeals and wins his appeal, then the situation reverts back to the point of service with the call becoming "short." If it was a first service, one more serve attempt is allowed. If the server already had one fault, this second fault would cause a side out.

(c) Double-bounce pick-up appeals. If the referee makes a call of "two bounces," thereby stopping play, the player against whom the call was made has the right of appeal, if he feels he retrieved the ball legally. If the appeal is upheld, the rally is re-played.

If the referee makes no call on a particular play during the course of a rally in which one player feels his opponent retrieved a ball on two or more bounces, the player feeling this way has the right of appeal.

However, since the ball is in play, the player wishing to appeal must clearly motion to the referee and linesmen, thereby alerting them to the exact play which is being appealed. At the same time, the player appealing must continue to retrieve and play the rally.

If the appealing player should win the rally, no appeal is necessary. If he loses the rally, and his appeal is upheld, the call is reversed and the "good" retrieve by his opponent becomes a "double-bounce pick-up," making the appealing player the winner of the rally and entitled to all benefits thereof.

Rule 3.10— If at any time during the course of a match the referee is of the opinion that a player or team is deliberately abusing the right of appeal, by either repetitive appeals of obvious rulings, or as a means of unsportsmanlike conduct, the referee shall enforce the Technical Foul rule.

Part IV. Play Regulations

Rule 4.1—Serve-Generally. (a) Order. The player or side winning the toss becomes the first server and starts the first game, and the third game, if any.

(b) Start. Games are started from any place in the service zone. No part of either foot may extend beyond either line of the service zone. Stepping on the line (but not beyond it) is permitted. Server must remain in the service zone until the served ball passes short line. Violations are called "foot faults."

(d) Manner. A serve is commenced by bouncing the ball to the floor in the service zone, and on the first bounce the ball is struck by the server's racquet so that it hits the front wall and on the rebound hits the floor back of the short line, either with or without touching one of the side walls.

(e) Readiness. Serves shall not be made until the receiving side is ready, or the referee has called play ball.

Rule 4.2—Serve-In Doubles. (a) Server. At the beginning of each game in doubles, each side shall inform the referee of the order of service, which order shall be followed throughout the game. Only the first server serves the first time up and continues to serve first throughout the game. When the first server is out—the side is out. Thereafter both players on each side shall serve until a hand-out occurs. It is not necessary for the server to alternate serves to their opponents.

(b) Partner's Position. On each serve, the server's partner shall stand erect with his back to the side wall and with both feet on the floor within the service box until the served ball passes the short line. Violations are called "foot faults."

Rule 4.3—Defective Serves. Defective serves are of three types resulting in penalties as follows:

(a) Dead Ball Serve. A dead ball serve results in no penalty and the server is given another serve without cancelling a prior illegal serve.

(b) Fault Serve. Two fault serves results in a hand-out.

(c) Out Serves. An out serve results in a hand-out.

Rule 4.4—Dead Ball Serves. Dead ball serves do not cancel any previous illegal serve. They occur when an otherwise legal serve:

(a) Hits Partner. Hits the server's partner on the fly on the rebound from the front wall while the server's partner is in the service box. Any serve that touches the floor before hitting the partner in the box is a short.

(b) Screen Balls. Passes too close to the server or the server's partner to obstruct the view of the returning side. Any serve passing behind the server's partner and the side wall is an automatic screen.

(c) Court Hinders. Hits any part of the court that under local rules is a dead ball.

Rule 4.5—Fault Serves. The following serves are faults and any two in succession results in a hand-out:

(a) Foot Faults. A foot fault results:

(1) When the server leaves the service zone before the served ball passes the short line.

(2) When the server's partner leaves the service box before the served ball passes the short line.

(b) Short Serve. A short serve is any served ball that first hits the front wall and on the rebound hits the floor in front of the back edge of the short line either with or without touching one side wall.

(c) Two-Side Serve. A two-side serve is any ball served that first hits the front wall and on the rebound hits two side walls on the fly.

(d) Ceiling Serve. A ceiling serve is any served ball that touches the ceiling after hitting the front wall either with or without touching one side wall.

(e) Long Serve. A long serve is any served ball that first hits the front wall and rebounds to the back wall before touching the floor.

(f) Out of Court Serve. Any ball going out of the court on the serve.

Rule 4.6—Out serves. Any one of the following serves results in a hand-out:

(a) Bounces. Bouncing the ball more than three times while in the service zone before striking the ball. A bounce is a drop or throw to the floor, followed by a catch. The ball may not be bounced anywhere but on the floor within the serve zone. Accidental dropping of the ball counts as one bounce.

(b) Missed Ball. Any attempt to strike the ball on the first bounce that results either in a total miss or in touching any part of the server's body other than his racquet.

(c) Non-front serve. Any served ball that strikes the server's partner, or the ceiling, floor or side wall, before striking the front wall.

(d) Touched Serve. Any served ball that on the rebound from the front wall touches the server, or touches the server's partner while any part of his body is out of the service box, or the server's partner intentionally catches the served ball on the fly.

(e) Out-of-Order Serve. In doubles, when either partner serves out of order.

(f) Crotch Serve. If the served ball hits the crotch in the front wall it is considered the same as hitting the floor and is an out. A crotch serve into the back wall is good and in play.

Rule 4.7—Return of Serve. (a) Receiving Position. The receiver or receivers must stand at least 5 feet back of the short line, as indicated by the 3-inch vertical line on each side wall, and cannot return the ball until it passes the short line. Any infraction results in a point for the server.

(b) Defective Serve. To eliminate any misunderstanding, the receiving side should not catch or touch a defectively served ball until called by the referee or it has touched the floor the second time.

(c) Fly Return. In making a fly return the receiver must end up with both feet back of the service zone. A violation by a receiver results in a point for the server.

(d) Legal Return. After the ball is legally served, one of the players on the receiving side must strike the ball with his racquet either on the fly or after the first bounce and before the ball touches the floor the second time to return the ball to the front wall either directly or after touching one or both side walls, the back wall or the ceiling, or any combination of those surfaces. A returned ball may not touch the floor before touching the front wall. (1) It is legal to return the ball by striking the ball into the back wall first, then hitting the front wall on the fly or after hitting the side wall or ceiling.

(e) Failure to Return. The failure to return a serve results in a point for the server.

Rule 4.8—Changes of Serve. (a) Hand-out. A server is entitled to continue serving until:

(1) Out Serve. He makes an out serve under Rule 4.6 or

(2) Fault Serves. He makes two fault serves in succession under

Rule 4.5, or

(3) Hits Partner. He hits his partner with an attempted return before the ball touches the floor the second time, or

(4) Return Failure. He or his partner fails to keep the ball in play by returning it as required by Rule 4.7(d), or

(5) Avoidable Hinder. He or his partner commits an avoidable hinder under Rule 4.11.

(b) Side-out (1) In Singles. In singles, retiring the server retires the side.

(2) In Doubles. In doubles, the side is retired when both partners have been put out, except on the first serve as provided in Rule 4.2(a).

(c) Effect. When the server on the side loses the serve, the server or serving side shall become the receiver; and the receiving side, the server; and so alternately in all subsequent services of the game.

Rule 4.9—Volleys. Each legal return after the serve is called a volley. Play during volleys shall be according to the following rules:

(a) One or both Hands. Only the head of the racquet may be used at any time to return the ball. The ball must be hit with the racquet in one or both hands. Switching hands to hit a ball is out. The use of any portion of the body is an out.

(b) One Touch. In attempting returns, the ball may be touched only once by one player on returning side. In doubles both partners may swing at, but only one may hit, the ball. Each violation of (a) or (b) results in a hand-out or point.

(c) Return Attempts. (1) In Singles. In singles if a player swings at but misses the ball in play, the player may repeat his attempts to return the ball until it touches the floor the second time.

(2) In Doubles. In doubles if one player swings at but misses the ball, both he and his partner may make further attempts to return the ball until it touches the floor the second time. Both partners on a side are entitled to an attempt to return the ball.

(3) Hinders. In singles or doubles, if a player swings at but misses the ball in play, and in his or his partner's attempt again to play the ball there is an unintentional interference by an opponent it shall be a hinder. (See Rule 4.10.)

(d) Touching Ball. Except as provided in Rule 4.10(a) (2), any touching of a ball before it touches the floor the second time by a player other than the one making a return is a point or out against the offending player.

(e) Out of Court Ball. (1) After Return. Any ball returned to the front wall which on the rebound or on the first bounce goes into the gallery or through any opening in a side wall shall be declared dead and the serve replayed.

(2) No Return. Any ball not returned to the front wall, but which caroms off a player's racquet into the gallery or into any opening in a side wall either with or without touching the ceiling, side or back wall, shall be an out or point against the players failing to make the return.

(f) Dry Ball. During the game and particularly on service every effort should be made to keep the ball dry. Deliberately wetting shall result in an out. The ball may be inspected by the referee at any time during a game.

(g) Broken Ball. If there is any suspicion that a ball has broken on the serve or during a volley, play shall continue until the end of the volley. The referee or any player may request the ball be examined. If the referee decides the ball is broken or otherwise defective, a new ball shall be put into play and the point replayed.

(h) Play Stoppage. (1) If a player loses a shoe or other equipment, or foreign objects enter the court, or any other outside interference occurs, the referee shall stop the play. (2) If a player loses control of his racquet, time should be called after the point has been decided, providing the racquet does not strike an opponent or interfere with ensuing play.

Rule 4.10—Dead Ball Hinders. Hinders are of two types—"dead ball" and "avoidable." Dead ball hinders, described in this rule, result in the point being replayed. Avoidable hinders are described in Rule 4.11.

(a) Situations. When called by the referee, the following are dead ball hinders:

(1) Court Hinders. Hits any part of the court which under local rules is a dead ball.

(2) Hitting Opponent. Any returned ball that touches an opponent on the fly before it returns to the front wall.

(3) Body Contact. Any body contact with an opponent that interferes with seeing or returning the ball.

(4) Screen Ball. Any ball rebounding from the front wall close to the body of a player on the side which just returned the ball, to interfere with or prevent the returning side from seeing the ball. See Rule 4.4(b).

(5) Straddle Ball. A ball passing between the legs of a player on the side which just returned the ball, if there is no fair chance to see or return the ball.

(6) Other Interference. Any other unintentional interference which prevents an opponent from having a fair chance to see or return the ball.

(b) Effect. A call by the referee of a "hinder" stops the play and voids any situation following, such as the ball hitting a player. No player is authorized to call a hinder, except on the back swing and such a call must be made immediately as provided in Rule 3.5(b).

(c) Avoidance. While making an attempt to return the ball, a player is entitled to a fair chance to see and return the ball. It is the duty of the side that has just served or returned the ball to move so that the receiving side may go straight to the ball and not be required to go around an opponent. The referee should be liberal in calling hinders to discourage any practice of playing the ball where an adversary cannot see it until too late. It is no excuse that the ball is "killed," unless in the opinion of the referee he couldn't return the ball. Hinders should be called without a claim by a player, especially in close plays and on game points.

(d) In Doubles. In doubles, both players on a side are entitled to a fair and unobstructed chance at the ball and either one is entitled to a hinder even though it naturally would be his partner's ball and even though his partner may have attempted to play the ball or that he may already have missed it. It is not a hinder when one player hinders his partner.

Rule 4.11—Avoidable Hinders. An avoidable hinder results in an "out" or a point depending upon whether the offender was serving or receiving.

(a) Failure to Move. Does not move sufficiently to allow opponent his shot.

(b) Blocking. Moves into a position effecting a block, on the opponent about to return the ball, or, in doubles, one partner moves in front of an opponent as his partner is returning the ball.

(c) Moving into Ball. Moves in the way and is struck by the ball just played by his opponent.

(d) Pushing. Deliberately pushing or shoving an opponent during a volley.

Rule 4.12—Rest Periods. (a) Delays. Deliberate delay exceeding ten seconds by server or receiver shall result in an out or point against the offender.

(b) During Game. During a game each player in singles, or each side in doubles, either while serving or receiving, may request a "time out" for a towel, wiping glasses, change or adjustment. Each "time out" shall not exceed 30 seconds. No more than three "time outs" in a game shall be granted each singles player or each team in doubles.

(c) Injury. No time out shall be charged to a player who is injured during play. An injured player shall not be allowed more than a total of 15 minutes of rest. If the injured player is not able to resume play after total rests of 15 minutes the match shall be awarded to the opponent or opponents. On any further injury to same player, the Commissioner, if present, or committee, after considering any available medical opinion shall determine whether the injured player will be allowed to continue.

(d) Between Games. A five-minute rest period is allowed between the first and second games and a 10-minute rest period between the second and third games. Players may leave the court between games, but must be on the court and ready to play at the expiration of the rest period.

(e) Postponed Games. Any games postponed by referee due to weather elements shall be resumed with the same score as when postponed.

Part V. Tournaments

Rule 5.1—Draws. The seeding method of drawing shall be the standard method approved by the U.S.R.A. and N.R.C. All draws in professional brackets shall be the responsibility of the National Director of the N.R.C.

Rule 5.2—Scheduling (a) Preliminary Matches. If one or more contestants are entered in both singles and doubles they may be required to play both singles and doubles on the same day or night with little rest between matches. This is a risk assumed on entering both singles and doubles. If possible the schedule should provide at least a one-hour rest period between all matches.

(b) Final Matches. Where one or more players have reached the finals in both singles and doubles, it is recommended that the doubles match be played on the day preceding the singles. This would assume more rest between the final matches. If both final matches must be played on the same day or night, the following procedure shall be followed:

(1) The singles match be played first.

(2) A rest period of not less than ONE HOUR be allowed between the finals in singles and doubles.

Rule 5.3—Notice of Matches. After the first round of matches, it is the responsibility of each player to check the posted schedules to determine the time and place of each subsequent match. If any change is made in the schedule after posting, it shall be the duty of the committee or chairman to notify the players of the change.

Rule 5.4—Third Place. In championship tournaments: national, state, district, etc. (if there is a playoff for third place), the loser in the semi-finals must play for third place or lose his ranking for the next year unless he is unable to compete because of injury or illness. See Rule 3.5(d) (4).

Rule 5.5—U.S.R.A. Regional Tournaments. Each year the United States and Canada are divided into regions for the purpose of sectional competition preceding the National Championships. The exact boundaries of each region are dependent on the location of the regional tournaments. Such locations are announced in NATIONAL RACQUET-BALL magazine.

(a) Only players residing in the area defined can participate in a regional tournament.

(b) Players can participate in only one event in a regional tournament.

(c) Winners of open singles in regional tournaments will receive round trip air coach tickets to the U.S.R.A. national tourney. Remuneration will be made after arrival at the Nationals.

(d) A U.S.R.A. officer will be in attendance at each regional tournament and will coordinate with the host chairman.

Awards: No individual award in U.S.R.A.-sanctioned tournaments should exceed value of more than $25.

Tournament Management: In all U.S.R.A.-sanctioned tournaments the tournament chairman and/or the national U.S.R.A. official in attendance may decide on a change of courts after the completion of any tournament game if such a change will accommodate better spectator conditions.

Tournament Conduct: In all U.S.R.A.-sanctioned tournaments the referee is empowered to default a match if an individual player or team conducts itself to the detriment of the tournament and the game.

Professional Definition: Any player who has accepted $200 or more in prizes and/or prize money in the most recent 12 calendar months is considered a professional racquetball player and ineligible for participation in any U.S.R.A.-sanctioned tournament bracket.

Amateur Definition: We hold as eligible for amateur racquetball tournaments sanctioned by the U.S.R.A. anyone except those who qualify as professionals under current U.S.R.A.-N.R.C. rules.

Pick-A-Partner: The essence of the "Players' Fraternity" has been to allow players to come to tournaments and select a partner, if necessary, regardless of what organization or city he might represent.

Age Brackets: The following age brackets, determined by the age of the player on the first day of the tournament, are:

Open: Any age can compete.

Juniors: 17 and under.

Seniors: 35 and over.

Masters: 45 and over.

Golden Masters: 55 and over.

In doubles both players must be within the specified age bracket.

ONE-WALL AND THREE-WALL RULES

Basically racquetball rules for one-wall, three-wall and four-wall are the same with the following exceptions:

One-Wall—**Court Size**—Wall shall be 20 ft. in width and 16 ft. high, floor 20 ft. in width and 34 ft. from the wall to back edge of the long line. There should be a minimum of 3 feet beyond the long line and 6 feet outside each side line. There should be a minimum of 6 feet outside each side line and behind the long line to permit movement area for the players.

Short Line—Back edge 16 feet from the wall. Service Markers—Lines at least 6 inches long parallel to and midway between the long and short lines, extending in from the side lines. The imaginary extension and joining of these lines indicates the service line. Lines are 1½ inches in width. Service Zone—floor area inside and including the short side and service lines. Receiving Zone—floor area in back of short line bounded by and including the long and side lines.

Three-Wall—**Serve**—A serve that goes beyond the side walls on the fly is player or side out. A serve that goes beyond the long line on a fly but within the side walls is the same as a "short."

GLOSSARY

Ace: A serve that touches the floor two or more times before the receiving player reaches it. One point is scored.

Avoidable Hinder: An avoidable interference of an opponent's clear shot; results in loss of serve or point.

Around-The-Wall Ball: A shot that, after hitting on the sidewall, rebounds to the front wall and to the opposite sidewall before it hits the floor.

Bum: Adjective used to describe your opponent if he has emerged victorious.

Back Court: The area of the court between the backwall and the receiving line.

Back-Wall Shot: Hitting the ball after it has rebounded off the back wall.

Ceiling Ball: A defensive shot striking the ceiling first, then the front wall, the floor, and rebounding into the back court.

Cross-Court Shot: A kill shot that travels from one side of the court to the other.

Cut-Spin: Adding control to a shot; also called under-spin or back-spin.

Cut-Throat: A game involving three players in which each player alternates playing against the other two players; each player keeps a separate score.

Defensive Shot: A shot that is made to keep the ball in play and avoid giving the opponent an opportunity for a kill shot.

Die: A hit so low and softly against a wall that it is virtually impossible to return.

Donut: A design left on your body after being hit with the ball by your opponent.

Doubles: A game played between two teams with two players per team.

Down-The-Wall Pass: A passing shot that travels along a sidewall.

Drive: A hard hit shot forcing your opponent to the back court.

Drop Shot: A shot hit so softly that it dies after hitting the front wall.

Error: Failure to return a playable ball.

Fault: An illegal serve or infraction of serving rules.

Front Court: The area of the court between the front wall and the service line.

Front Wall-Side Wall Kill: A kill shot that, after hitting the front wall, rolls out from the sidewall.

Game Point: When the server is serving for the point to win the game.

Garbage Serve: A medium-arc serve to the back court, forcing the receiver to hit a return shot at shoulder level.

Hinder: Blocking a player's fair chance to see and return the ball.

Inning: A round of play in which both players complete serving.

Kill Shot: An offensive shot hit so low on the front wall that it is impossible to return.

Lob Serve: A high-arc serve to the back court.

Match: Competition consisting of two out of three games.

Middle Court: The area of the court between the service line and the receiving line.

Optimum Court Position: Approximately the center of the court with your opponent behind you.

Overhead Drive: A hard-hit drive shot using a stroke similar to a tennis serve.

Overhead Kill: A low percentage kill shot like an overhead drive.

Pass Shot: A hard-hit shot past an opponent and beyond the player's reach.

Pinch Shot: A front wall-sidewall kill.

Plum: An easy kill shot.

Rally: An exchange of shots.

Roll Out: A perfect kill shot that strikes the front wall so low it rebounds with no bounce.

Screen: Blocking an opponent's view by being too close to a ball in play.

Serve: The shot that begins play.

Setup: A shot made easily when an opponent makes a mistake or poor judgment.

Side-Out: Loss of serve.

Throat: The part of the racquet between the strings and the grip.

V Pass: A passing shot traveling in a V path.

Volley: A ball hit on the fly.

Z Ball: A shot hitting the front wall, sidewall and opposite sidewall on the fly.

A PERSONAL WORD FROM MELVIN POWERS
PUBLISHER, WILSHIRE BOOK COMPANY

Dear Friend:

My goal is to publish interesting, informative, and inspirational books. You can help me accomplish this by answering the following questions, either by phone or by mail. Or, if convenient for you, I would welcome the opportunity to visit with you in my office and hear your comments in person.

Did you enjoy reading this book? Why?

Would you enjoy reading another similar book?

What idea in the book impressed you the most?

If applicable to your situation, have you incorporated this idea in your daily life?

Is there a chapter that could serve as a theme for an entire book? Please explain.

If you have an idea for a book, I would welcome discussing it with you. If you already have one in progress, write or call me concerning possible publication. I can be reached at (213) 875-1711 or (213) 983-1105.

Sincerely yours,

MELVIN POWERS

12015 Sherman Road
North Hollywood, California 91605

MELVIN POWERS SELF-IMPROVEMENT LIBRARY

ASTROLOGY

_____ASTROLOGY: A FASCINATING HISTORY *P. Naylor*	2.00
_____ASTROLOGY: HOW TO CHART YOUR HOROSCOPE *Max Heindel*	3.00
_____ASTROLOGY: YOUR PERSONAL SUN-SIGN GUIDE *Beatrice Ryder*	3.00
_____ASTROLOGY FOR EVERYDAY LIVING *Janet Harris*	2.00
_____ASTROLOGY MADE EASY *Astarte*	2.00
_____ASTROLOGY MADE PRACTICAL *Alexandra Kayhle*	3.00
_____ASTROLOGY, ROMANCE, YOU AND THE STARS *Anthony Norvell*	4.00
_____MY WORLD OF ASTROLOGY *Sydney Omarr*	4.00
_____THOUGHT DIAL *Sydney Omarr*	3.00
_____ZODIAC REVEALED *Rupert Gleadow*	2.00

BRIDGE

_____BRIDGE BIDDING MADE EASY *Edwin B. Kantar*	5.00
_____BRIDGE CONVENTIONS *Edwin B. Kantar*	4.00
_____BRIDGE HUMOR *Edwin B. Kantar*	3.00
_____COMPETITIVE BIDDING IN MODERN BRIDGE *Edgar Kaplan*	4.00
_____DEFENSIVE BRIDGE PLAY COMPLETE *Edwin B. Kantar*	10.00
_____HOW TO IMPROVE YOUR BRIDGE *Alfred Sheinwold*	2.00
_____INTRODUCTION TO DEFENDER'S PLAY *Edwin B. Kantar*	3.00
_____TEST YOUR BRIDGE PLAY *Edwin B. Kantar*	3.00
_____WINNING DECLARER PLAY *Dorothy Hayden Truscott*	4.00

BUSINESS, STUDY & REFERENCE

_____CONVERSATION MADE EASY *Elliot Russell*	2.00
_____EXAM SECRET *Dennis B. Jackson*	2.00
_____FIX-IT BOOK *Arthur Symons*	2.00
_____HOW TO DEVELOP A BETTER SPEAKING VOICE *M. Hellier*	2.00
_____HOW TO MAKE A FORTUNE IN REAL ESTATE *Albert Winnikoff*	3.00
_____INCREASE YOUR LEARNING POWER *Geoffrey A. Dudley*	2.00
_____MAGIC OF NUMBERS *Robert Tocquet*	2.00
_____PRACTICAL GUIDE TO BETTER CONCENTRATION *Melvin Powers*	2.00
_____PRACTICAL GUIDE TO PUBLIC SPEAKING *Maurice Forley*	3.00
_____7 DAYS TO FASTER READING *William S. Schaill*	3.00
_____SONGWRITERS RHYMING DICTIONARY *Jane Shaw Whitfield*	5.00
_____SPELLING MADE EASY *Lester D. Basch & Dr. Milton Finkelstein*	2.00
_____STUDENT'S GUIDE TO BETTER GRADES *J. A. Rickard*	2.00
_____TEST YOURSELF—Find Your Hidden Talent *Jack Shafer*	2.00
_____YOUR WILL & WHAT TO DO ABOUT IT *Attorney Samuel G. Kling*	3.00

CALLIGRAPHY

_____CALLIGRAPHY—The Art of Beautfiul Writing *Katherine Jeffares*	5.00

CHESS & CHECKERS

_____BEGINNER'S GUIDE TO WINNING CHESS *Fred Reinfeld*	3.00
_____BETTER CHESS—How to Play *Fred Reinfeld*	2.00
_____CHECKERS MADE EASY *Tom Wiswell*	2.00
_____CHESS IN TEN EASY LESSONS *Larry Evans*	2.00
_____CHESS MADE EASY *Milton L. Hanauer*	2.00
_____CHESS MASTERY—A New Approach *Fred Reinfeld*	2.00
_____CHESS PROBLEMS FOR BEGINNERS *edited by Fred Reinfeld*	2.00
_____CHESS SECRETS REVEALED *Fred Reinfeld*	2.00
_____CHESS STRATEGY—An Expert's Guide *Fred Reinfeld*	2.00
_____CHESS TACTICS FOR BEGINNERS *edited by Fred Reinfeld*	2.00
_____CHESS THEORY & PRACTICE *Morry & Mitchell*	2.00
_____HOW TO WIN AT CHECKERS *Fred Reinfeld*	2.00
_____1001 BRILLIANT WAYS TO CHECKMATE *Fred Reinfeld*	3.00
_____1001 WINNING CHESS SACRIFICES & COMBINATIONS *Fred Reinfeld*	3.00
_____SOVIET CHESS *Edited by R. G. Wade*	3.00

COOKERY & HERBS

_____CULPEPER'S HERBAL REMEDIES *Dr. Nicholas Culpeper*	2.00
_____FAST GOURMET COOKBOOK *Poppy Cannon*	2.50
_____HEALING POWER OF HERBS *May Bethel*	3.00

———HEALING POWER OF NATURAL FOODS *May Bethel*	3.00
———HERB HANDBOOK *Dawn MacLeod*	2.00
———HERBS FOR COOKING AND HEALING *Dr. Donald Law*	2.00
———HERBS FOR HEALTH—How to Grow & Use Them *Louise Evans Doole*	2.00
———HOME GARDEN COOKBOOK—Delicious Natural Food Recipes *Ken Kraft*	3.00
———MEDICAL HERBALIST *edited by Dr. J. R. Yemm*	3.00
———NATURAL FOOD COOKBOOK *Dr. Harry C. Bond*	3.00
———NATURE'S MEDICINES *Richard Lucas*	3.00
———VEGETABLE GARDENING FOR BEGINNERS *Hugh Wiberg*	2.00
———VEGETABLES FOR TODAY'S GARDENS *R. Milton Carleton*	2.00
———VEGETARIAN COOKERY *Janet Walker*	3.00
———VEGETARIAN COOKING MADE EASY & DELECTABLE *Veronica Vezza*	2.00
———VEGETARIAN DELIGHTS—A Happy Cookbook for Health *K. R. Mehta*	2.00
———VEGETARIAN GOURMET COOKBOOK *Joyce McKinnel*	3.00

GAMBLING & POKER

———ADVANCED POKER STRATEGY & WINNING PLAY *A. D. Livingston*	3.00
———HOW NOT TO LOSE AT POKER *Jeffrey Lloyd Castle*	3.00
———HOW TO WIN AT DICE GAMES *Skip Frey*	3.00
———HOW TO WIN AT POKER *Terence Reese & Anthony T. Watkins*	2.00
———SECRETS OF WINNING POKER *George S. Coffin*	3.00
———WINNING AT CRAPS *Dr. Lloyd T. Commins*	2.00
———WINNING AT GIN *Chester Wander & Cy Rice*	3.00
———WINNING AT POKER—An Expert's Guide *John Archer*	3.00
———WINNING AT 21—An Expert's Guide *John Archer*	3.00
———WINNING POKER SYSTEMS *Norman Zadeh*	3.00

HEALTH

———DR. LINDNER'S SPECIAL WEIGHT CONTROL METHOD	1.50
———HELP YOURSELF TO BETTER SIGHT *Margaret Darst Corbett*	3.00
———HOW TO IMPROVE YOUR VISION *Dr. Robert A. Kraskin*	2.00
———HOW YOU CAN STOP SMOKING PERMANENTLY *Ernest Caldwell*	2.00
———MIND OVER PLATTER *Peter G. Lindner, M.D.*	2.00
———NATURE'S WAY TO NUTRITION & VIBRANT HEALTH *Robert J. Scrutton*	3.00
———NEW CARBOHYDRATE DIET COUNTER *Patti Lopez-Pereira*	1.50
———PSYCHEDELIC ECSTASY *William Marshall & Gilbert W. Taylor*	2.00
———REFLEXOLOGY *Dr. Maybelle Segal*	2.00
———YOU CAN LEARN TO RELAX *Dr. Samuel Gutwirth*	2.00
———YOUR ALLERGY—What To Do About It *Allan Knight, M.D.*	2.00

HOBBIES

———BATON TWIRLING—A Complete Illustrated Guide *Doris Wheelus*	4.00
———BEACHCOMBING FOR BEGINNERS *Norman Hickin*	2.00
———BLACKSTONE'S MODERN CARD TRICKS *Harry Blackstone*	2.00
———BLACKSTONE'S SECRETS OF MAGIC *Harry Blackstone*	2.00
———BUTTERFLIES	2.50
———COIN COLLECTING FOR BEGINNERS *Burton Hobson & Fred Reinfeld*	2.00
———ENTERTAINING WITH ESP *Tony 'Doc' Shiels*	2.00
———400 FASCINATING MAGIC TRICKS YOU CAN DO *Howard Thurston*	3.00
———GOULD'S GOLD & SILVER GUIDE TO COINS *Maurice Gould*	2.00
———HOW I TURN JUNK INTO FUN AND PROFIT *Sari*	3.00
———HOW TO PLAY THE HARMONICA FOR FUN AND PROFIT *Hal Leighton*	3.00
———HOW TO WRITE A HIT SONG & SELL IT *Tommy Boyce*	7.00
———JUGGLING MADE EASY *Rudolf Dittrich*	2.00
———MAGIC MADE EASY *Byron Wels*	2.00
———STAMP COLLECTING FOR BEGINNERS *Burton Hobson*	2.00
———STAMP COLLECTING FOR FUN & PROFIT *Frank Cetin*	2.00

HORSE PLAYERS' WINNING GUIDES

———BETTING HORSES TO WIN *Les Conklin*	3.00
———ELIMINATE THE LOSERS *Bob McKnight*	3.00
———HOW TO PICK WINNING HORSES *Bob McKnight*	3.00
———HOW TO WIN AT THE RACES *Sam (The Genius) Lewin*	3.00
———HOW YOU CAN BEAT THE RACES *Jack Kavanagh*	3.00
———MAKING MONEY AT THE RACES *David Barr*	3.00

METAPHYSICS & OCCULT

SELF-HELP & INSPIRATIONAL

___ MENTAL POWER THROUGH SLEEP SUGGESTION *Melvin Powers*		2.00
___ NEW GUIDE TO RATIONAL LIVING *Albert Ellis, Ph.D. & R. Harper, Ph.D.*		3.00
___ OUR TROUBLED SELVES *Dr. Allan Fromme*		3.00
___ PRACTICAL GUIDE TO SUCCESS & POPULARITY *C. W. Bailey*		2.00
___ PSYCHO-CYBERNETICS *Maxwell Maltz, M.D.*		2.00
___ SCIENCE OF MIND IN DAILY LIVING *Dr. Donald Curtis*		2.00
___ SECRET POWER OF THE PYRAMIDS *U. S. Andersen*		4.00
___ SECRET OF SECRETS *U. S. Andersen*		4.00
___ STUTTERING AND WHAT YOU CAN DO ABOUT IT *W. Johnson, Ph.D.*		2.50
___ SUCCESS-CYBERNETICS *U. S. Andersen*		4.00
___ 10 DAYS TO A GREAT NEW LIFE *William E. Edwards*		3.00
___ THINK AND GROW RICH *Napoleon Hill*		3.00
___ THREE MAGIC WORDS *U. S. Andersen*		4.00
___ TREASURY OF THE ART OF LIVING *Sidney S. Greenberg*		5.00
___ YOU ARE NOT THE TARGET *Laura Huxley*		3.00
___ YOUR SUBCONSCIOUS POWER *Charles M. Simmons*		4.00
___ YOUR THOUGHTS CAN CHANGE YOUR LIFE *Dr. Donald Curtis*		3.00

SPORTS

___ ARCHERY—An Expert's Guide *Dan Stamp*		2.00
___ BICYCLING FOR FUN AND GOOD HEALTH *Kenneth E. Luther*		2.00
___ BILLIARDS—Pocket • Carom • Three Cushion *Clive Cottingham, Jr.*		2.00
___ CAMPING-OUT 101 Ideas & Activities *Bruno Knobel*		2.00
___ COMPLETE GUIDE TO FISHING *Vlad Evanoff*		2.00
___ HOW TO WIN AT POCKET BILLIARDS *Edward D. Knuchell*		3.00
___ LEARNING & TEACHING SOCCER SKILLS *Eric Worthington*		3.00
___ MOTORCYCLING FOR BEGINNERS *I. G. Edmonds*		2.00
___ PRACTICAL BOATING *W. S. Kals*		3.00
___ RACQUETBALL MADE EASY *Steve Lubarsky, Rod Delson & Jack Scagnetti*		3.00
___ SECRET OF BOWLING STRIKES *Dawson Taylor*		2.00
___ SECRET OF PERFECT PUTTING *Horton Smith & Dawson Taylor*		3.00
___ SECRET WHY FISH BITE *James Westman*		2.00
___ SKIER'S POCKET BOOK *Otti Wiedman* (4¼" x 6")		2.50
___ SOCCER—The game & how to play it *Gary Rosenthal*		2.00
___ STARTING SOCCER *Edward F. Dolan, Jr.*		2.00
___ TABLE TENNIS MADE EASY *Johnny Leach*		2.00

TENNIS LOVERS' LIBRARY

___ BEGINNER'S GUIDE TO WINNING TENNIS *Helen Hull Jacobs*		2.00
___ HOW TO BEAT BETTER TENNIS PLAYERS *Loring Fiske*		4.00
___ HOW TO IMPROVE YOUR TENNIS—Style, Strategy & Analysis *C. Wilson*		2.00
___ INSIDE TENNIS—Techniques of Winning *Jim Leighton*		3.00
___ PLAY TENNIS WITH ROSEWALL *Ken Rosewall*		2.00
___ PSYCH YOURSELF TO BETTER TENNIS *Dr. Walter A. Luszki*		2.00
___ SUCCESSFUL TENNIS *Neale Fraser*		2.00
___ TENNIS FOR BEGINNERS *Dr. H. A. Murray*		2.00
___ TENNIS MADE EASY *Joel Brecheen*		2.00
___ WEEKEND TENNIS—How to have fun & win at the same time *Bill Talbert*		3.00
___ WINNING WITH PERCENTAGE TENNIS—Smart Strategy *Jack Lowe*		2.00

WILSHIRE PET LIBRARY

___ DOG OBEDIENCE TRAINING *Gust Kessopulos*		3.00
___ DOG TRAINING MADE EASY & FUN *John W. Kellogg*		2.00
___ HOW TO BRING UP YOUR PET DOG *Kurt Unkelbach*		2.00
___ HOW TO RAISE & TRAIN YOUR PUPPY *Jeff Griffen*		2.00
___ PIGEONS: HOW TO RAISE & TRAIN THEM *William H. Allen, Jr.*		2.00

The books listed above can be obtained from your book dealer or directly from Melvin Powers. When ordering, please remit 30¢ per book postage & handling. Send for our free illustrated catalog of self-improvement books.

Melvin Powers
12015 Sherman Road, No. Hollywood, California 91605

181-6	AMATEUR HORSE BREEDER *A. C. Leighton Hardman*	3.00
237-5	AMERICAN QUARTER HORSE IN PICTURES *Margaret Cabell Self*	3.00
182-4	APPALOOSA HORSE *Donna & Bill Richardson*	3.00
183-2	ARABIAN HORSE *Reginald S. Summerhays*	2.00
273-1	ART OF WESTERN RIDING *Suzanne Norton Jones*	3.00
184-0	AT THE HORSE SHOW *Margaret Cabell Self*	3.00
185-9	BACK-YARD FOAL *Peggy Jett Pittinger*	3.00
186-7	BACK-YARD HORSE *Peggy Jett Pittinger*	3.00
219-7	BASIC DRESSAGE *Jean Froissard*	2.00
284-7	BEGINNER'S GUIDE TO HORSEBACK RIDING *Sheila Wall*	2.00
271-5	BEGINNER'S GUIDE TO THE WESTERN HORSE *Natlee Kenoyer*	2.00
231-6	BITS—THEIR HISTORY, USE AND MISUSE *Louis Taylor*	3.00
272-3	BREAKING & TRAINING THE DRIVING HORSE *Doris Ganton*	2.00
334-7	BREAKING YOUR HORSE'S BAD HABITS *W. Dayton Sumner*	3.00
222-7	CAVALRY MANUAL OF HORSEMANSHIP *Gordon Wright*	3.00
235-9	COMPLETE TRAINING OF HORSE AND RIDER *Colonel Alois Podhajsky*	4.00
281-2	DISORDERS OF THE HORSE & WHAT TO DO ABOUT THEM *E. Hanauer*	2.00
028-3	DOG TRAINING MADE EASY & FUN *John W. Kellogg*	2.00
187-5	DRESSAGE—A Study of the Finer Points in Riding *Henry Wynmalen*	4.00
242-1	DRIVING HORSES *Sallie Walrond*	2.00
316-9	ENDURANCE RIDING *Ann Hyland*	2.00
188-3	EQUITATION *Jean Froissard*	4.00
189-1	FIRST AID FOR HORSES *Dr. Charles H. Denning, Jr.*	2.00
190-5	FUN OF RAISING A COLT *Rubye & Frank Griffith*	2.00
191-3	FUN ON HORSEBACK *Margaret Cabell Self*	4.00
329-0	GYMKHANA GAMES *Natlee Kenoyer*	2.00
302-9	HORSE DISEASES—Causes, Symptoms & Treatment *Dr. H. G. Belschner*	3.00
192-1	HORSE OWNER'S CONCISE GUIDE *Elsie V. Hanauer*	2.00
193-X	HORSE SELECTION & CARE FOR BEGINNERS *George H. Conn*	3.00
209-X	HORSE SENSE—A complete guide to riding and care *Alan Deacon*	4.00
229-4	HORSEBACK RIDING FOR BEGINNERS *Louis Taylor*	4.00
194-8	HORSEBACK RIDING MADE EASY & FUN *Sue Henderson Coen*	3.00
195-6	HORSES—Their Selection, Care & Handling *Margaret Cabell Self*	3.00
279-0	HOW TO BUY A BETTER HORSE & SELL THE HORSE YOU OWN	3.00
280-4	HOW TO ENJOY YOUR QUARTER HORSE *Williard H. Porter*	3.00
253-7	HUNTER IN PICTURES *Margaret Cabell Self*	2.00
241-3	ILLUSTRATED BOOK OF THE HORSE *S. Sidney* (8½" x 11½")	10.00
210-3	ILLUSTRATED HORSE MANAGEMENT—400 Illustrations *Dr. E. Mayhew*	5.00
240-5	ILLUSTRATED HORSE TRAINING *Captain M. H. Hayes*	5.00
196-4	ILLUSTRATED HORSEBACK RIDING FOR BEGINNERS *Jeanne Mellin*	2.00
197-2	JUMPING—Learning & Teaching *Jean Froissard*	3.00
294-4	KNOW ALL ABOUT HORSES *Harry Disston*	3.00
308-8	LAME HORSE—Causes, Symptoms & Treatment *Dr. James R. Rooney*	3.00
202-2	LAW & YOUR HORSE *Edward H. Greene*	4.00
198-0	LIPIZZANERS & THE SPANISH RIDING SCHOOL *W. Reuter* (4¼" x 6")	2.50
359-2	MANUAL OF HORSEMANSHIP *Harold Black*	5.00
236-7	MORGAN HORSE IN PICTURES *Margaret Cabell Self*	2.00
274-X	MOVIE HORSES—The Fascinating Techniques of Training *Anthony Amaral*	2.00
199-9	POLICE HORSES *Judith Campbell*	2.00
239-1	PRACTICAL GUIDE TO HORSESHOEING	2.00
292-8	PRACTICAL GUIDE TO OWNING YOUR OWN HORSE *Steven D. Price*	2.00
247-2	PRACTICAL HORSE PSYCHOLOGY *Moyra Williams*	3.00
200-6	PROBLEM HORSES Guide for Curing Serious Behavior Habits *Summerhays*	2.00
333-9	REINSMAN OF THE WEST—BRIDLES & BITS *Ed Connell*	4.00
225-1	RESCHOOLING THE THOROUGHBRED *Peggy Jett Pittenger*	3.00
252-9	RIDE WESTERN *Louis Taylor*	2.00
201-4	SCHOOLING YOUR YOUNG HORSE *George Wheatley*	2.00
258-8	STABLE MANAGEMENT FOR THE OWNER-GROOM *George Wheatley*	4.00
297-9	STALLION MANAGEMENT—A Guide for Stud Owners *A. C. Hardman*	3.00
227-8	TEACHING YOUR HORSE TO JUMP *W. J. Froud*	2.00
203-0	TRAIL HORSES & TRAIL RIDING *Anne & Perry Westbrook*	2.00
335-5	TRAINING YOUR HORSE TO SHOW *Neale Haley*	3.00
255-3	TREATING COMMON DISEASES OF YOUR HORSE *Dr. George H. Conn*	3.00
230-8	TREATING HORSE AILMENTS *G. W. Serth*	2.00
285-5	WESTERN HORSEBACK RIDING *Glen Balch*	2.00
204-9	WONDERFUL WORLD OF PONIES *Peggy Jett Pittenger* (8½" x 11½")	4.00
360-6	YOU AND YOUR PONY *Pepper Mainwaring Healey* (8½" x 11")	6.00
251-0	YOUR FIRST HORSE *George C. Saunders, M.D.*	3.00
331-2	YOUR PONY BOOK *Hermann Wiederhold*	2.00
205-7	YOUR WESTERN HORSE *Nelson C. Nye*	2.00

*The books listed above can be obtained from your book dealer or directly from
Melvin Powers. When ordering, please remit 30c per book postage & handling.
Send for our free illustrated catalog of self-improvement books.*

Melvin Powers

12015 Sherman Road, No. Hollywood, California 91605

NOTES

NOTES

NOTES

NOTES